"Cindy Spring has harn
to the soul as we face
in the loss of a loved on
death, these stories can help us befriend the great mystery of existence. Don't wait! There is something for everyone in this book."

Frances Vaughan, Ph.D. Author, *Shadows of the Sacred:*
Seeing through Spiritual Illusions

"This short, easy to read, extensively researched collection of stories is itself a story. It is the story of humanity needing to make meaning out of human existence. Those looking for comfort will find it not only in the convergence of understandings of the nature of death, but in the examples of how many have faced it in ways that brought acceptance and fulfillment."

Leonard Joy Quaker Institute for the Future Board of Trustees

"In a short, clear and concentrated book, Cindy Spring gives us many gifts: important stories, deep quotes and poetry, insights into many spiritual traditions and many delicious, if challenging, concepts about death to consider. It's a treasure trove of heart and information, food for living and elixir for dying."

Kate Munger Founder, Threshold Choir

"Stories can soothe an ailing soul, give meaning to our experiences, answer the unanswerable, and offer comfort in times of uncertainty and mourning. I am thankful to Cindy Spring for offering us this precious collection of stories on death and the afterlife she respectfully lifted up from different world spiritual traditions. She guides us with grace and insight, asking us to consider their multiple truths. I found solace reading this book, and I will gift it to friends in times of uncertainty and mourning."

Gabriella Lettini, Ph.D. Dean of the Faculty at Starr King School
for the Ministry, Graduate Theological Union;
Aurelia Henry Reinhardt Professor of Theological Ethics

"Among the many books on death and dying that have poured into our culture in the past 30 years, *The Wave and The Drop* is unique. In this breathtaking and profound collection of wisdom stories about death drawn from many diverse human traditions, Cindy Spring offers us the whole of human wisdom on the journey to the edge of life and beyond. Her stories are relevant for us all, offering us a compass for the unknown and healing fear into a sense gratitude and peace. One of the most important books I have read, both professionally and personally."

Rachel Naomi Remen, M.D. Author, *Kitchen Table Wisdom* and
My Grandfather's Blessings

"Touching, helpful, healing and wise! These are the words that well up as I read Cindy Spring's moving gift of the world's wisdom stories that millions of people have used to guide their lives and ease their deaths. This is a book that will enrich anyone who wants to live fully and all of us who may someday die."

Roger Walsh M.D., Ph.D. Professor of psychiatry, University of California; Author of *Essential Spirituality: The Seven Central Practices*

"In my experience, what we believe about what happens after death may shape the way in which we die and even the way in which we live our lives. *The Wave and The Drop* engages us in a profound inquiry into this Mystery."

Frank Ostaseski Author, *The Five Invitations: Discovering What Death Can Teach Us About Living Fully*; Founder, Metta Institute

"I love your book. It means more than I can say to be part of your holding circle around this great small package of wisdom, truth, and story. So many things resonate for me. I want to give copies to many friends after it is published."

Elisabeth Belle Friend of author and
member of book support circle

The Wave and The Drop

Wisdom Stories about Death and Afterlife

Cindy Spring

Wisdom Circles Publishing

Wisdom Circles Publishing
1063 Leneve Place
El Cerrito, CA 94530
www.cindyspring.com
wave@cindyspring.com

For complete list of permissions for quoted materials,
please see "Permissions" (pp. 151-152)

Cover graphic: Jane Hayes

Typesetting and Design: Margaret Copeland, Terragrafix
www.terragrafix.com

Publishing consultant: Naomi Rose
www.writingfromthedeeperself.com

Proofreading: Gabriel Steinfeld gstein@sonic.net

Line drawings by Naomi Rose, www.naomirose.net

Author photograph taken by Stu Selland

Social Science/Death & Dying SOC 036000;
Religion/Inspiration REL 036000

Printed in the United States of America

First printing 2018

ISBN: 978-0-9996989-0-7

Dedicated to

Charles Garfield, my soulmate,
whose love and support infuse this book

And to our parents,
Chick and Rita Centkowski
Ed and Sylvia Garfield
who taught us so much
about Living and Dying

Table of Contents

Foreword by Charles Garfield, Ph.D.

At 93, my indomitable mother suffered a devastating stroke. After several nerve-wracking weeks, she was moved to the skilled nursing floor at St. Paul's Towers, an Oakland senior residence, where she'd been living on her own. Now diagnosed with congestive heart failure, Mom was significantly impaired, under heavy medication and mostly bed-ridden. Nonetheless, I was jolted by the doctor's comment that she had less than six months to live.

With heavy spirits, we arranged for round-the-clock care, and Mom agreed to enter a hospice program with a surprising lack of drama. Thereafter, her little room had a constant flow of nurses, hospice personnel, and family, including her grandchildren — my brother Jon's kids, Teddy and Hannah — in whose company she delighted. It was clear that, even in this grim situation, Mom loved receiving all our love and attention.

"You won't be on your own in the weeks ahead," I promised her. "The family will be with you." I hugged her gently, feeling her frail shoulder blades, and hoping she wouldn't see my tears. "And I'll be your partner for the journey."

As a young clinical psychologist, I had cared for older people suffering quietly and alone at the UCSF Cancer Institute and the VA hospital in San Francisco. In 1974, there were only a handful of counselors and psychologists to help the thousands who were facing terminal illnesses alone. That year, I founded the Shanti Project to teach others how to provide practical and emotional support to people in their dying time. Over the past 43 years, we've trained 18,000 volunteers, and, with the help of Shanti, some 20,000 individuals have found partners for their dying time.

Over the years, my work in the field of death and dying has earned its share of accolades. More importantly, I learned a great deal about supporting people through emotional and spiritual end-of-life transitions. But this death was going to be up close and personal. Would the teacher fail the test? Could I apply all the insights I'd passed on to clients and colleagues to my own mother?

As Mom's physical condition deteriorated, her dying morphed from a family tragedy into a mysterious adventure. Our conversations deepened. Each day seemed to offer her a possible initiation, a glimpse of a new reality. As time went by, Mom episodically entered some illuminated place, some heaven very different from her everyday world. In these moments of grace, she became very loving and opened her heart to us. The miracle was that she started living more richly and deeply in the middle of her dying process.

Waking abruptly one afternoon, Mom stared wide-eyed toward the foot of her bed. "There's my father, right there!" she exclaimed. "Pop's come to see me. He's standing with a crowd of people. I know them all."

"Who are they?"

"My mother is here, smiling at me!" Incredulity rang in her voice. "I just taught her how to thread a needle — she's very pleased!"

This vision helped to ground her psychologically in the weeks ahead. "It was thrilling to have company," she said, now that we were once again the only two people in the room.

Like my mother, many people experience "visits" from loved ones long dead. Is this the mind's attempt to smooth the way? Are these people some kind of psychic escort? Or are they guardian angels, as some traditions hold? These questions are yet another aspect of the Mystery.

The time I spent with Mom in her final days provided some of our richest memories. My sadness was mixed with profound gratitude that she'd been in my life for so long. Drifting in and out of consciousness, she'd suddenly turn to me and say, "I love you so much." Mom now looked translucent, peaceful, otherworldly, as if she'd been dipping into a reality far greater than the one she'd inhabited for her nine decades here on earth.

During those last months, Mom had a conversation with my wife Cindy, asking her, "What do you think happens when we die?" The question welled up from the center of her soul, as Mom grappled with her fear of death and of the unknown, and she urgently needed an answer. Intuitively, Cindy reached for a wisdom story — The Wave and The Drop — and helped my mother envision the next stage of her journey. Their conversation in her dying time was the seed for this wise and comforting book.

Wisdom stories can help people who are facing the end of life and want to put it in the deepest, and most accommodating, frame. In the chapters that follow, you will find tales of transcendence, wholeness and reconciliation that can help you consider your own mortality, zero in on what gives your life the greatest meaning, and intuit where it is you're heading. Drawn from a variety of traditions, these stories can be a wonderful source of solace and comfort for you, and for loved ones who are entering their dying time — and they can provide a touchstone for heart-full discussion with friends and family.

In these pages, I hope you will find your own personal wisdom story — the one that resonates with your soul and helps you think about your own endings and beginnings. My wish is that everyone who reads this book will feel the sense of love and connection that my mother discovered in her final days from the story of the wave and the drop.

— Charles Garfield, Ph.D.
April, 2017

Introduction

In the fall of 2009, I was sitting in the kitchen with my husband's mother, Sylvia. The two of us knew she had only months to live. Out of the blue, she turned to me and asked, "What happens when we die?"

I could have turned the question back on her. "I don't know. What do you think?" But she was counting on me for support. I had been "the daughter she never had" for nearly 30 years. So I took a deep breath and out came my answer, unrehearsed.

"Well, we don't know for sure, but we do have stories about this rite of passage from many different cultures. I think each one of them contains a grain of truth."

I added that my mother and father, both lifelong Roman Catholics, believed in heaven. After a life of hard work and generous contributions to their community, they felt they had earned such a reward.

"Tell me some stories," Sylvia said.

I told her three stories that I hoped might offer solace. The one she latched onto was The Wave and The Drop. In this Hindu tale, a single drop of water is thrown from a wave. For a brief moment, this little drop has a life of its own. Then it falls back into the wave and rejoins the movement of the ocean. Sylvia liked the simplicity of this story, and the notion of returning to the primordial waters, the source of life. During the time my mother-in-law was confined to a skilled nursing facility, she referred to The Wave and The Drop several times. She described how much she liked the feeling of being a drop falling back into the ocean. Each time she mentioned this, she relaxed a bit more.

Being present during the dying time of family members and friends, I have seen firsthand how important it is to have stories, images, and perhaps certain selections of music, that are attempts to capture an essence of what happens at the time of death and afterward. I was struck by the thought that everyone should have a good story to ride out on. Why not compile a book of tales from around the world, a kind of "Aesop's Fables" for the dying time? Such a book might also serve as a "toe in the water" for those just starting to contemplate their own mortality. It might also help us carry on a conversation about a prospect that everyone faces, when words are hard to find.

This book brings together some of the most universal stories about death, afterlife, and transformation. Every tribe, religion, and culture on the planet has evolved its own stories. In this book, the sources are referred to as *wisdom traditions,* and their stories as *wisdom stories.* Some describe entering a white light, others foretell a reuniting with the source of life, or promise a new dimension such as heaven or nirvana. Sometimes the dying person sees escorts: deceased parents, or a spouse, angels, and other transcendent figures, ready to assist in the transition from life to death. Elements common to all of these stories are Love, Light, and Communion.

You may feel drawn to this book because you're hoping to find a story to illuminate your journey thus far, and also looking for a sense of how it might look at the end. It may offer you a shelter where you can rest quietly, and consider those questions about life and death that keep lurking in the shadows, questions that won't go away. Or perhaps someone you love is dying and you want to offer them a wisdom story. Either way, this book will introduce you to new ways of thinking about death and the afterlife.

What happens *when* we die?

What happens *after* we die?

We humans have been grappling with these questions for a very long time. According to cultural anthropologists, our early ancestors were more concerned with the survival of the community, and the continuity of the generations. Somewhere along the way, we started to wonder more about what happens to the individual after death. Because humans have diverse cultures on this planet, we have a variety of stories about dying and death. We now have access to the wisdom of these cultures to draw upon for our own use.

Are things heard at Christian memorial services such as "He's with God now," or "She's in a place free of pain," true or fanciful? Are there escorts, as Sufis say, waiting to help us in the transition? It is said in Tibetan Buddhism that beliefs may shape our entrance into nonphysical reality. We'll consider these and other ways of holding death and afterlife.

Fear of Death

Fear of death is normal. It's instinctive — watch any predator/prey encounter. All animals, including humans, react with fear when threatened. When did humans begin to fear death without any clear and present danger? The story is captured in the Jewish Old Testament in Genesis: Eve defies God's instructions. She eats the apple and suddenly humans are cast out of Paradise, and know both suffering and death. Buddhists refer to this awareness as discovering the truth of impermanence. Indigenous peoples view individual death as a way of participating in the Circle of Life.

Cultural historian Arnold Toynbee divided afterlife stories into three broad categories. In the first, the individual personality persists after the body perishes. "An overwhelming majority of mankind, in all places and at all times since our ancestors awakened to consciousness, has held that [the human] personality is not annihilated at death," he wrote.

In other stories, we lose our individuality and become part of some greater whole. Toynbee said that in this view, "the human personality is a temporary detached splinter… at death, [it] is reabsorbed into the spiritual reality that is its source." That source is sometimes referred to as an "Ocean of Love," which fits well with The Wave and The Drop story.

In still another category, the personality is extinguished and we simply "fade to black." This is the story currently embraced by mainstream science. If you receive a terminal diagnosis, a doctor can offer an "educated guess" about how long you may live that can be helpful, and unnerving. Even with all of its major advances on how to extend life, modern medicine offers us scant advice on how to live with a terminal diagnosis. This is why we need to reclaim other stories about the dying time — a time that can be lonely and painful. They give us a way to view our final days, and more than that, they can give shape and meaning to the arc of an entire life.

Why has almost every culture and religious tradition sought to provide a story about the afterlife? I'd like to suggest one explanation: In our short stay here, we explore many forms of love, revel in our moments of joy and discovery, and experience a sense of purpose and accomplishment. The loss of all of that is a staggering challenge. Life-after-death stories comfort us with the promise of continuation, and they comfort those left behind with the promise of reunion. They also confirm our deep knowing that there is something beyond physical reality.

As the short story writer Barry Lopez said, "Sometimes a person needs a story more than food." This is especially true in the dying time, when food becomes much less interesting. Having a story to "hang your hat on" can ease your fears and help others accept your passing. Each day, every day, approximately 153,000 humans die. Catastrophic events around the globe are adding to this toll. Here in the US, the numbers are swelling as the Boomer generation ages. Will you be in that number tomorrow? Next year, or twenty years from now? How much time do you have left before it's *your day*? Can you imagine letting go without sadness or fear?

For many, these ultimate questions are hard to entertain. But stories can help us to consider this scenario, and cope with a range of difficult emotions. Each story I present opens up a way of holding the humbling thought that we are mortal.

Our gift, and our curse, is knowing that we will die someday. Usually we start with the negatives. We find it easy to conjure up death's terrors. We need to be reminded of contemplating its virtues: how we are making way for the next generation, how it gives us an opportunity to review our memories, and a time to step back from the pace of daily life to find its deeper meaning. As these stories show, death may be the final step in our maturation process, and a time for fashioning our greatest legacy. Does your chosen story inform the way you live? It does, you know. If you believe that too many sins will land you in purgatory, it serves as a moral code. If you believe that service to others (being a bodhisattva in Buddhism) is the ultimate path to nirvana, you'll try to live accordingly. If you have a story, does it sustain you in times of grief? Can you draw strength from it?

The sense of an ending deepens our appreciation of the present moment, our sense of the preciousness of our existence. When we are deeply aware of own mortality, we live with more compassion for others, more awareness of the beauty and sorrow around us, and more freedom from the fear of our own day of passing on. Our story also serves as a place of solace on those dreadful days when we lose a loved one.

Nurses and counselors report that even people who insist they are prepared for death often feel a sudden terror about what happens next. What we *think* we believe may not sustain us during our dying. When American spiritual teacher Ram Dass had a massive stroke in 1997, he was surprised by his own reaction. "What's extraordinary," he said, "is that I did not have a spiritual thought. Here I am, 'Mr. Spiritual,' and in my own death, I didn't orient towards the spirit. It shows me that I have some work to do...I flunked the test." Ram Dass returned from that threshold and continues his work, now with greater humility. His courage to carry on, in spite of limitations to his speaking ability, is inspiring.

The specter of death can provoke great anxiety, not just at the end of life, but any time we stop to think about our own mortality. In his book *Staring at the Sun*, psychiatrist Irvin D. Yalom examines our deep-seated fear of death:

> As we reach the crest of life and look at the path before us, we apprehend that the path no longer ascends but slopes downward toward decline and diminishment. From that point on, concerns about death are never far from mind.

Over four decades, Yalom has treated individuals for whom "the fear of death erupts into terror that negates all happiness and fulfillment." These aren't people who are at death's door, or suffering from a terminal illness, yet they carry a nagging fear that something is about to happen that will erase them from this earth. Yalom concludes, "Hidden and disguised, leaking out in a variety of symptoms, it [death] is the wellspring of many of our worries, stresses and conflicts."

Storytelling

For more than half a million years, members of our human lineage have been sitting in circles around campfires. Imagine listening to the sounds of carnivores echoing in the darkness. Someone begins to tell a story to keep fear at bay. Having a story that helps us come to terms with death lessens the fear of dying, and contributes to our sense of psychological well-being — at any point in life. You may have a story that has served you since childhood, a tale passed down from generation to generation. Or you may find comfort in a story that you learned as an adult. Either way, that story has become your guide. You may hold it as a belief, or as a deep knowing, or carry it lightly as a hope. Through the ages, Truth often dresses up as Story.

This is what the wisdom traditions tell us: We enter the world from Mystery and we return to Mystery. And in the interim, we develop a narrative to make sense of life. All along the way, we tell stories. Stories form the bedrock of a culture and contain its wisdom. So it's not surprising that a story can help steady the mind as the body slows down and the ego senses its demise. For some people, a worn out or pain-wracked body is a prison and they long for release. Others sense the end is near, and insist on all manner of physical and prayerful interventions to forestall the inevitable. Stories help us tap into some inner wisdom that knows when it's time to let go.

Counselor Kathleen Dowling Singh, who was present at hundreds of hospice deaths, has witnessed the dying time become, for some people, an "opportunity to move into a deeper apprehension of the nature of reality." Every culture has its stories that tell of saintly people who approach death as a threshold experience. They say their goodbyes with smiling faces and appear to relax into an acceptance of what's to come, a trust that they're going to be held and received by some larger force. Yet others feel indignant at the prospect of fading from this earth, like Welsh poet Dylan Thomas, who advised, "Do not go gentle into that dark night. Rage, rage against the dying of the light." Can you predict how you will respond, when it's your time?

In writing this book, I did not set out to explore a particular tradition in depth. My goal was simply to gather stories that reflect the essence of a tradition, not its history as a religion. These stories will help us consider the mystery of life and death. They may also help start conversations with a loved one whose death seems unthinkable to us. Or the dying person may want very much to have such a conversation, but a spouse or family member cannot approach the subject.

Some of the stories I've chosen are from classic sources. Where possible, I drew on contemporary stories that relay the wisdom of the tradition. Alongside traditional stories about heaven, you'll find recent accounts of near-death experiences. In the chapter on the ancient belief in reincarnation, I've included a couple of contemporary stories about children who seem able to recall past lives with amazing detail. The cyclical nature of Life and Death is captured in Native American stories. Also considered is the choice to "die with dignity," that is, to end your life on your own terms. And we'll see that some traditions hold that a transcendent union with the Infinite is the goal of all earthly spiritual practice, not survival of an individual personality. Pausing on the threshold between life and death requires courage, whether or not you believe in an afterlife, as I do. I hope you find a story in this book that holds you during your dying time, just as The Wave and The Drop did for Sylvia Garfield.

Sometimes you don't need an entire story — just a poem or a brief selection from a longer essay can help you weave your own. In the Tapestry section, you'll find a selection of inspiring quotes from seekers such as Rumi, Emily Dickinson, and Kahlil Gibran.

Wisdom stories have power because they provide explanations for the existence of Life and Death. They have been shared over centuries, by millions of people. Stories are a seawall against our limited lifespan. When we share them with a whole community, we feel better equipped to step outside our usual death-denying world and open to a different point of view. My story allows me to stare down death — like the Stanford engineering professor on his deathbed who told his loved ones: "I'm off to my next great adventure."

Our wisdom stories are also evolving. Over time, they have been colored and shaped by each culture, and by the place where they were told. The heaven described by an ancient Chinese philosopher is different from the heaven found in a Negro spiritual. So much of Life is ineffable — love, grief, beauty, loss, grace. So too, is death. No one story can capture it. A story points the way to the Mystery, the way a finger points to the moon.

When Death knocks on your door, will you be ready? Will you be prepared with a story if you need it? It's hard to tell from a distance, when you think you have time left. What you do know is that the sea level is rising — slowly, perceptibly. This book is an invitation to test the waters.

The Story of The Wave and The Drop

A wave crashes on the shore. A drop is thrown high into the air, separated momentarily from the ocean, alive with waves and swells. The drop has its brief existence, then falls back into the welcoming waters.

What could be more simple? Ocean. Wave. A spray of drops cast high into the sunshine, each one distinctly individual. Then the descent back into the wave, back into ocean, the abiding whole. This story of Life as a cycle of oneness and separateness comes from Hindu philosophy, the oldest existing spiritual tradition that has written texts, with roots going back over 5,000 years.

For ocean-bordering countries, like India, water is a gateway to a vast territory. The image of water as a source for wisdom is universal. Could it be because water comprises 60 percent of the human body, and 71 percent of the surface of the earth? Water is also a symbol for the

Unconscious. The wave holds infinite possibilities for individual drops to form.

Hindu teachings say that during our separation as a drop, we become aware of our existence as an individual self and all that it entails: curiosity, ambition, joy, attraction, desire, loneliness, pain, disappointment, loss. Then the drop that is my self is reunited with Ocean.

A Story of Continuation or Annihilation?

The story of the wave and the drop suggests that the goal of the personality is to merge with the cosmos — that our individuality is meant to be extinguished. Yet Hinduism also embraces the belief in reincarnation — the notion that we get many lifetimes in which to hone our character and awareness. In its vast literature, the Hindu tradition holds both annihilation and continuation — stories about the death and rebirth of the individual.

As Huston Smith, author of *The Illustrated World's Religions,* observes, "Hindu literature is full of parables and metaphors designed to open our imaginations to this infinite which lies concealed in the depths of everyday life." Not to worry if they contradict each other. One reason Hindu philosophy can encompass this seeming contradiction is because it contains so many variations.

This spiritual tradition embraces at least six separate systems of thought. One of them, the Yogic system, has at least four different paths of attaining union with the Divine. Union through the body, familiar to many of us as Hatha-Yoga, is one of the four. Jnana-Yoga is the path of wisdom; Karma-Yoga, the path of work and service; and Bhakti-Yoga, the path that cultivates love and devotion.

In Hindu tradition, *there are many paths,* and many different manifestations of the Divine. Some are benevolent, like Rama, revered for his compassion. Ganesh is recognizable from his elephant head, and is said to be the remover of obstacles. But there are also violent deities like Durga, who governs creation and annihilation, and her offshoot, Kali, the goddess who destroys evil forces. A ten-day festival to honor Durga is held annually in many parts of India.

Hindu cosmology, while enormous, holds insights that are simple and available to us all. As we'll see throughout this book, there are those who seek God's company after death, and those who anticipate merging with God. Hindu tradition captures all the stories. The Ocean contains the Drop. The Drop contains the Ocean… .

From *Parables of Rama*:

A drop of water in the shape of a tear fell from the clouds. The tear fell, and when asked, "Why this weeping?" It replied "O, I am such a tiny, puny, insignificant thing. I am so small, Oh too small, and the ocean is so big. I weep at my smallness." It was told, "Weep not, do not confine yourself to name and form only, but look within you; see what you are. Are you not water, and what is the ocean? Is it not water too? Things which are equal to the same thing are equal to one another. Don't look at yourself as being confined in space and time. Look beyond this Space and Time, and see your Reality.

The 13th-century Sufi mystic and poet Rumi put it this way:

You are not a drop in the ocean, you are the entire ocean in a drop.

Wave and Drop, Vibration and Form, Heaven and Earth…these could all be taken as pointing toward the same ineffable reality. The opening of Genesis in the Judeo-Christian Bible, King James Version (KJV) is: "In

the beginning God created the heaven and the earth...."
Author and teacher Neil Douglas-Klotz has translated
early sacred writings from Aramaic and Hebrew and
tries to capture the essence of what the texts mean in
their native language and cultural setting. In his book,
Desert Wisdom, he finds a deeper meaning in the original Hebrew.

Instead of using the English word *heaven*, he translates
the word *shamayim* as "the ocean of light, sound, name
and vibration" — a limitless expanse of waves with no
boundaries.

In place of the usual translation of *aretz* as *earth*, he
translates it as "the cosmic tendency toward the Limited,"
which comes in the form of discrete entities, particles, or
individuals.

Vibration and form. Energy and Matter. To see the
creation of the universe as a manifestation of the wave and
drop may be closer to the original intent of the ancient
author of Genesis.

As I Dissolve...

In 2009, Rabbi Zalman Schachter-Shalomi, founder
of the Jewish Renewal Movement, embarked upon a
project when he knew he had only a few years to live. He

asked a writer to help him compile some guidance on "how to prepare for the mystery." With Sara Davidson, he created *The December Project*, a summary of the wisdom he acquired through a lifetime of digging into the roots of Judaism and not being confined by its orthodoxy.

They compiled a series of 12 short exercises to help us face our own mortality. One is the practice of letting go of our identification with the body and instead, seeing it as a separate entity. As Reb Zalman said, when he was in pain: "Poor Zalman's flesh. You've been so useful, so dependable; you've carried me so well. I'm sorry you are not comfortable right now."

Reb Zalman also spoke about dissolving like a drop of water, as he prepared to leave his body. This is what we're told he said, shortly before he passed away:

> It's as if the body and soul are tied together with little strings. The closer you get to leaving, the more the strings loosen and the more you connect with greater awareness, the expanded mind.... I want to watch the last breath going out and whisper the Shema. I want to merge back with the infinite; I want to dissolve like a drop of water in the greater ocean.

There are many paths. Other traditions offer alternative ways of looking at death and afterlife. As we shall see, the message that comes through all the wisdom traditions is that the visible world we live in and the invisible world of Spirit are in continuous interaction. Listening to the stories in this book can inform us on how to approach death when the time comes.

The Story of Heaven

I had been at the hospital with a client for seven nights straight, a man I had not met before. A friend of his had called me because he knew that I did this kind of volunteer vigil-keeping. The dying man was terrified, especially of dying alone. He had been too weak to talk. He just wanted to see a face whenever he opened his eyes.

At about four in the morning he was struggling for each breath. I wanted it to be over as much for myself as for him. I wanted a shot of Jameson's, a hot bath and bed in that order. I was standing by his bed holding his hand. Suddenly he gripped my hand with amazing strength. His eyes opened wide and asked: "Am I alright with God?"

My mind started racing with thoughts — "I'm not a priest." "I don't know this man's religious background." "What should I say?" He repeated: "Am I alright with God?"

There was a moment of absolute silence that seemed to absorb even the machine beeps and wheezes, the mucus rattling in his throat. I felt my body and the hospital room fill with love. Palpable. Textured. Alive. I looked into his eyes and said with a smile: "You are so loved."

His face cleared. His eyes gentled. He died.

~

Peggy Flynn told me her story of being with this stranger during his dying time. She was able to tap into her Irish Catholic upbringing, her extensive experience with hospice work, and most of all, her love for the teachings of Jesus. She brought all that into the hospital room in order to truthfully answer his question with: "You are so loved."

The Story of Heaven is the story of the gathering of the beloved community on earth and in a dimension beyond our ordinary reality. A homecoming. Everyone is welcome. Peggy believes that there may be "repair and rehab work" to do after death, but no one is left out.

Peggy Flynn was born into a family that extended far back into Christian and Celtic roots. She recalled when she was a little girl asking her grandmother who would sometimes sit off by herself, "Why are you sitting by yourself, instead of with all of us?" Her grandmother answered, "I'm not alone. I'm with my dead." The reality of a permeable veil between this life and the next was part of her family culture.

I was introduced, as Peggy was, to the Story of Heaven in the 1950s, in a Catholic school. All children were given a copy of the Baltimore Catechism, a book of short questions and answers based on Catholic doctrine.

Why did God make me?
God made me to know Him, to love Him, and to serve Him in this world, and to be happy with Him forever in heaven.

The catechism also taught that God existed within each individual, and that belief was reinforced for me at every Sunday Mass by the ritual of Holy Communion. When I received the wheat wafer on my tongue that had been transmuted by the priest into the Body of Christ, I lost my sense of self. For a minute or two, Christ was in me, I was in Christ. A truly transcendent experience. That gift of personal connection is why many Catholics choose to receive Holy Communion on their deathbed.

Tom Henry was also raised in a Catholic family. He told me his dad had always impressed him with his belief in going to heaven after death. When the father was in his dying time, he told the family that he was looking forward to meeting some of the people he had admired all his life, including George Washington and Abraham Lincoln. Amidst the sadness, Tom's father promised the family that they would all be reunited in heaven and that he was going to pave the way.

Tom is currently director of the "contemporary music" Sunday service at his Lutheran church. He chooses songs from well known folk singers such as James Taylor's *Home by Another Way*. He says, "My role as music director gives me great joy and deepens my sense of participation in this world and the next."

Sometimes reunion in heaven is all you have to hold onto when a loved one is dying. When I was fifteen years old, my Catholic faith became a life raft in a sea of sadness. My dear cousin Paula had just completed her freshman year at Rosary High School in Detroit when she was diagnosed with kidney disease. The doctors assured the family there was a "99 percent chance" that someone her age would recover. But she got sicker and sicker. Paula and I were very devoted to Mary, the mother of Jesus. Day after day as she lay in her hospital bed, I would say the rosary for her. Paula died that summer and was carried to heaven on the whispers of thousands of Hail Mary's. I have no doubt she made it there. It's been over fifty years since she passed. I still have that blue crystal rosary.

The creation of the "beloved community" is described in the Gospel of Luke where he says Jesus reminds us that no one is ever truly lost:

> What man of you, having a hundred sheep, if he has lost one of them, does not leave the ninety-nine in the open country, and go after the one that is lost, until he finds it? And when he has found it, he lays it on his shoulders, rejoicing. And when he comes home, he calls together his friends and his neighbors, saying to them, "Rejoice with me, for I have found my sheep that was lost." (Luke 15:4-7)

This concern for the individual as a member of the beloved community, especially someone who has been marginalized or ostracized, has been given new life by Pope Francis. In his book, *Pilgrimage: My Search for the Real Pope Francis*, biographer Mark Shriver tells stories of when Francis (then Jorge Mario Bergoglio) was

Archbishop of Buenos Aires. Shriver visited Argentina and interviewed a woman on the street who was a prostitute with three children. She told Shriver that the archbishop had often given her food, but what she was truly grateful for was that he always addressed her as *Senorita*, a term of honor. Another story tells of how Francis invited a garbage collector from Argentina to be in the front row at his Papal Inauguration in 2013. Francis reminds us of the lesson in the Gospel of Matthew: "*I was hungry and you gave me meat; I was thirsty and you gave me drink; I was a stranger and you took me in.... Inasmuch as ye have done it unto one of the least of my brethren, ye have done it unto me.*"

Heaven Bound

The wisdom traditions of Christianity and Islam both emphasize a one-to-one relationship with God or Allah that culminates in heaven. This singular relationship was embraced by the Egyptians at least 4600 years ago. At that time, worthy rulers were thought to be invited at their death by Re, the sun god, to join the deities in the sky.

The king ascends to the sky among the gods dwelling in the sky.... "The arriver comes!" say the gods. Re gives thee his arm on the stairway to the sky.

"He who knows his place comes," say the gods. O Pure One, assume thy throne in the barque of Re and sail thou the sky.

As the Egyptian belief in the afterlife evolved over the millennia, more and more individuals were thought to attain heaven if they passed the judgment of the god Osiris who lived in the underworld.

The promise of heaven is also found in Chinese mythology dating back to the 12th-century BCE. *Tian*, the word that stands for heaven, was a place where ancestors reside along with an over-arching supreme deity. But it was more than just a place. Heaven was an active force, said to watch over all people, blessing those who were pleasing, and sending calamities to those who were offensive. The Temple of Heaven consists of three magnificent buildings constructed in the early 1400s in what is now Beijing. It continues to be a place of prayer and supplication, where people go to seek a blessing.

In the Judeo-Christian Bible, heaven is described as a paradise in the desert, a field of plenty or a grove of fruit trees, with bees making honey, grazing sheep, murmuring fountains and streams.

The Islamic story of heaven or paradise (called Jannah) is similar: a bountiful and happy place, where "every wish is immediately fulfilled." The Quran, the holy book of Islam, links the righteous path to heaven with actions that promote truth and justice:

> Allah will say: This is a day in which the truthful will profit from their truth. Theirs are gardens, with rivers flowing beneath — their eternal Home. Allah is well-pleased with them, and they with Allah. That is the great salvation. (5:119)

The Story of Heaven would not be complete without a mention of the Story of Hell. Both Christianity and Islam describe in their classic writings an afterlife place of eternal damnation. People "in hell" are those who have separated themselves from communion with the One (God or Allah). Souls are there by virtue of having consistently chosen behaviors such as extreme greed and hatred, without repentance. Some, but not all, contemporary theologians in both religions hold that because the divine being is all-merciful, hell cannot be eternal. Those in hell keep getting signals that they are still loved. They can try to suppress or ignore those signals, but only for so long.

When the message begins to get through, the invitation to rejoin the One becomes clear.

A Band of Angels

Music can hold wisdom stories beautifully...

> *If you get there before I do*
> *Comin' for to carry me home*
> *Tell all my friends I'm a-comin' too*
> *Comin' for to carry me home*

This verse comes from what is perhaps the best-known Negro spiritual, *Swing Low Sweet Chariot.* It's still sung in many churches today. Gospel music was built on the hope of reuniting decimated families and communities in heaven. The multi-part harmonies and call-and-response lyrics in Gospel music stem from African oral traditions — allowing slaves to hold on to a portion of their culture deeply rooted in community. As African-American theologian Howard Thurman noted, the teachings of Jesus speak to all who are oppressed and to those with their backs against the wall.

Songs containing comforting images such as "comin' home," "crossing a river," and "taking flight" are found in the repertoire of The Threshold Choir, founded by Kate Munger in the year 2000 in Northern California. Small groups of two to four singers respond to a request from a dying person or family member, or from someone on the hospice team, to come to the bedside. Munger says she started the choir because "singing is an ancient practice that tribal humans do for one another when someone is struggling. A song can be a bridge from the purely physical, temporal experience to what lies beyond." This story from their website captures the mission of the group:

> In the early summer of 2011, my sister entered hospice care and was confined to her bed with cancer. I called a friend in Threshold Choir and asked if the choir would come and sing to her. It was a beautiful and loving time. The singers came each Friday for six or seven weeks. Each week, different family members and friends would come to be with my sister and listen. We were connected by the beautiful harmony of the loving, soft, and gentle voices. The Threshold Choir singing added dignity to one of life's saddest events. Sometimes people do not want to hear that someone they love is dying. But the singers were active witnesses

to what was happening. It gave me a chance to be on my sister's journey for a short time and to bless her and let her travel alone.

As of 2017, there were over 150 chapters of the Threshold Choir around the world. There is no charge for their services. Each Threshold group draws upon a repertoire of songs, many composed by choir members — such as Helen Greenspan's "Ocean's Breath," Katharine Osburn's "Remember Me," and Laura Fannon's "My Grateful Heart." Founder Kate Munger composed a simple song, inspired by a line from the spiritual teacher Ram Dass: "We're all just walking each other home," sung over and over in different harmonies. When possible the choir will also sing requested popular songs such as "Some Enchanted Evening," "Sentimental Journey," or "Shenandoah." Music weaves its way through our lives and certain songs become touchstones for positive memories. Which songs would you pick to hear during your dying time?

We never know what someone's "perfect" song may be at life's end. Not long ago, singers came to be with a lifelong baseball fan who had requested "Take Me Out to the Ballgame." As the group sang the line, "One... two...

three strikes you're out," she breathed her last breath and passed on to the big green field in the sky.

The appeal and staying power of The Story of Heaven is clear. It gives us a compelling promise of personal immortality, along with the hope of transcending suffering. It gives us a moral code that underscores the values of charity and service to community. And it strengthens our connection with loved ones: "I'll see you again in heaven." It's no wonder that a billion Christians and a billion Muslims hold it as a core tenet of their faith. In a recent Pew Research survey, 72 percent of American adults answered "yes" to the question: "Do you believe in heaven?"

Historian Arnold Toynbee suggested another role that belief in an afterlife serves. He says that heaven promises humans that we are participants in a world that "is not confined to the physical, mental and temporal limits of a human lifetime, but is adequate spiritually to man's spiritual potentiality." In other words, life may be limited here on earth by the constraints of survival and procreation, but in heaven we will be able to be fully ourselves with no constraints. The gift of consciousness has allowed us to know that no matter how abundant or inadequate our circumstances, most of us feel "there's more to me than this." The hope that we may reach that potential in an afterlife, or in a reincarnation, or in another form of existence, keeps us aspiring to reach that ideal.

This chapter presents the Story of Heaven as handed down through the ages. We'll continue it in the next chapter, as told by individuals who describe it from the vantage point of a near-death experience.

Stories of Near-Death Experiences

Something had appeared in the darkness. Turning slowly, it radiated fine filaments of white light, and as it did so, the darkness around began to splinter and break apart. Then I heard a new sound, a living sound, like the richest, most complex, most beautiful piece of music you've ever heard. Growing in volume as a pure white light descended, it obliterated the monotonous mechanical pounding that, seemingly for eons, had been my only company up until then.

The light got closer and closer, spinning around and around and generating those filaments of pure white light that I now saw were tinged, here and there, with hints of gold. Then, at the very center of the light, something else appeared. I focused my awareness, hard, trying to figure out what it was. An opening. I was no longer looking at the slowly spinning light at all, but through it. The moment I understood this, I began to move up. Fast. There was a whooshing sound, and in a flash I went through the opening and found myself in a completely new world. The strangest, most beautiful world I'd ever seen.

Brilliant, vibrant, ecstatic, stunning... I could heap on one adjective after another to describe what this world looked and felt like, but they'd all fall short. I felt like I was being born. Not reborn, or born again. Just... born.

In his book, *Proof of Heaven*, neurosurgeon Eben Alexander describes his frightening journey through a dark tunnel. At the end he comes upon a brilliant white light, and radiant figures introduce him to a strange and beautiful world. These are some of the classic elements of the near-death experience or NDE.

Dr. Alexander had been diagnosed with a severe case of bacterial meningitis. Even after days of extraordinary medical measures, he slipped into a deep coma. When a week passed with no sign of improvement, the attending physician suggested that it was time to let him go. This is how he explained it to Dr. Alexander's wife: If we unplug him from the ventilator, and he survives, he's very likely going to remain in a "vegetative state" for the rest of his life. The news was grim, but she held out, and her husband

miraculously woke up. After many months of rehabil-
itation, including learning how to speak again, he gave a
vivid description of his "time away."

In heaven, he met the Girl on the Butterfly Wing who
told him that his life on earth was not complete. His wife
and two sons still needed him and he had important work
to do. He didn't know then that the work included writing
a bestselling book about this near-death encounter that
would inspire millions of people.

In recent years, tens of thousands of stories of NDEs
have been recorded and archived. These accounts include
testimonies from people expected to die within a day or
so, and those pronounced "clinically dead" who described
visiting "another realm" that felt very real to them.

Perhaps the earliest known version of an NDE is in
St. Paul's second letter to the Corinthians, in the New
Testament:

> I know a man in Christ who fourteen years ago
> was caught up to the third heaven. Whether it was
> in the body or out of the body I do not know —
> God knows. And I know that this man — whether
> in the body or apart from the body I do not know,
> but God knows — was caught up to paradise and

heard inexpressible things, things that no one is permitted to tell. (Corinthians 2 12:2-4)

Stories of near-death experiences have been included in this volume, not because they constitute a story to hold onto, but because the description offers us another glimpse of what the experiencer often calls heaven, or a dimension where one could sort things out. Some NDE accounts do not include a journey to a "heavenly place," but can also activate the will to live. In *Between Life & Death*, Sheldon Ruderman describes a terrifying inner journey after surgery for heart cancer:

Grotesque forms paraded before my eyes. Undefined, unfamiliar, nightmarish horrors. They seemed to be all over the room. ... By now it had become obvious to me that the doctors had done all they could, but that they simply did not know enough to save my life. I was more and more sure that the question of survival would have to be decided in some other arena, and that it had something to do with my understanding of this mind-space.

Ruderman enters a kind of purgatory where several scenarios are played out. "I debated whether it was worth continuing the fight [to live]," he writes, "or whether I should just close my eyes and drift off to a long, long rest, out of this maelstrom. Just how much was I willing to endure to retain this tortured state of life? Each time the question seemed to answer itself. I got an image of being in a room, backing up to a door behind me. If I kept going, I would go through the door and be out of life. Standing in front of the door, however, was my small son, Jason. To back out the door, I would have to step on him or push him out of the way. I could not do that." Ruderman chose to opt for life.

Common Elements

NDEs have been studied by researchers, mainly psychologists, for over a hundred years. In 1892, a distinguished Swiss geology professor, Albert Heim, published a report describing the subjective experiences of people who survived severe falls in the Alps. Based on over thirty accounts, he claimed that nearly every one of his interviewees recalled that they had no anxiety, time greatly expanded, mental activity became enormous and the person falling "often heard beautiful music and fell in a superbly blue heaven containing roseate cloudlets."

Let's not forget that these NDEs are stories from people in their dying time, some who were in coma, severe trauma, or had been declared dead by doctors. What's common to all of them is the sense that they "went somewhere." For them, it was firsthand evidence that the spirit continues after death. Most accounts contain some version of "it was such a wonderful place, filled with light and love, I didn't want to return to my body." But return they did, eager to describe their own view of heaven and the afterlife. Those who tell their NDE stories in books say that they have a deeper appreciation of life and a greatly diminished fear of death.

Eben Alexander's book set off a new wave of popular interest in the NDE. We now have an avalanche of similar books (over 50 published in 2015), all trying to answer the question: Is heaven for real? In 2013, CNN broadcast a popular program, *To Heaven and Back,* featuring Mary Neal, a surgeon and kayaker, who was declared dead after being pulled from a whitewater rafting disaster. Later she recounted being trapped underwater: "I could feel bones breaking. I could feel ligaments and the tissue tearing. I felt my spirit peeling away from my body." She described visiting a domed structure exploding not only with light and color but with love. She talked with spirits who told her it was not her time to die and she returned to life.

Also featured was Anita Moorjani, who was told she had less than two days to live because her virulent cancer was shutting down her organs. She went into a coma. Later she described a scene where she remembered her husband and loved ones gathered around her bedside along with her deceased father and others she didn't know. She felt and heard their love for her. She said she had a moment of clarity where she realized her lifelong feelings of being flawed had manifested as cancer. She had witnessed her best friend Soni ravaged and killed by cancer. In Anita's coma, Soni was at her bedside. Anita decided to come back to realize who she truly was. Her organs began to function again and within five weeks there was no evidence of cancer in her body. She has since written several books and given a TED talk.

NDEs have provided plenty of grist for contemporary researchers. In 2014, an international study focused on 2,060 people who survived cardiac arrest. About nine percent described inner journeys consistent with NDEs. Two percent had explicit recall of these events. Researchers suggest that more subjects had heightened mental activity as they neared death, but lost their memories after recovery (through brain damage or heavy medication). But a great majority of people who survive a brush with death tell of no such adventures.

What can we make of the stories about this portal to the afterlife, a place filled with vast, unimagined energies? Whether it exists only "in the imagination," or in another dimension of existence, remains a mystery.

The Story of Reincarnation

Light and free you let go, darling, forward and up. You are going forward and up; you are going toward the light. Willing and consciously you are going, willingly and consciously, and you are doing this beautifully; you are doing this so beautifully — you are going toward the light; you are going toward a greater love; you are going forward and up…. You are doing it so beautifully, so easily. Light and free…. You are going toward a greater love than you have ever known. You are going towards the best, the greatest love, and it is easy, it is so easy, and you are doing it so beautifully.

These loving words were spoken into the ear of Aldous Huxley, at his prior request, by his wife, Laura Huxley, in the last hours of his life. According to Laura Huxley, she kept repeating the words of the prayer from the *Tibetan Book of the Dead* along with her own words of encouragement, until Aldous stopped breathing at 5:20 p.m. on November 22, 1963. Huxley was the author of

Brave New World, and had one of the most brilliant minds of the 20th century. In his monumental work, *The Perennial Philosophy*, Huxley respectfully examined and synthesized the classic wisdom traditions. In his words, he searched for "the one divine Reality substantial to the manifold world of things and lives and minds." For his own crossing of the threshold, he chose to follow the story from Tibetan Buddhism.

In this tradition, passing from this life is seen as a crucial moment in our spiritual development, and it offers many useful insights. One is that everything in the universe is impermanent, subject to continuous change. Another is that one must consciously prepare for death and for transition to the next life on earth, or reincarnation. Preparation helps to make the transition easier, and the goal is to do this consciously and with grace. *The Tibetan Book of the Dead* offers to help us quell anxiety and fear. Here's another prayer from this source:

> You are dying, you are leaving your friends and family, your favorite surroundings will no longer be there, you are going to leave us. But at the same time there is something which continues, there is continuity of your positive relationship with your

friends and with the teachings, so work on that basic continuity, which has nothing to do with ego. When you die you will have all sorts of traumatic experiences, of leaving the body, as well as your old memories coming back to you as hallucinations. Whatever the visions and hallucinations may be, just relate to what is happening, rather than trying to run away. Keep there, just relate with that.

In Buddhism, it is believed that most people who die go through a process of *reincarnation*, that is, a being dies and then at some point, begins a new life in a different physical body or form. This belief was held in such diverse places as Hellenistic Greece and the land of the Druid Celts. In Buddhism, the spiritual principle of *karma* determines the next reincarnation. Every action has consequences: good intentions and good deeds contribute to good karma, and harmful intentions and deeds contribute to bad karma. The karma of past lives affects the current one as well as future lives.

The story of Buddhism begins with Siddhartha Gautama, who lived in northern India, around 2,500 years ago. Siddhartha was born into a wealthy Hindu family and sheltered from the ordinary world. At age twenty-nine, he went outside the walls of his family compound for the first time and encountered the suffering of many people. He watched a cremation. He was so moved that he chose to renounce his wealth and live the life of a holy man. He meditated and studied with various teachers. One day he sat under the Bodhi (enlightenment) tree and vowed to remain there until he was enlightened. There he liberated himself from the cycles of death and rebirth. Enlightenment is one of those difficult-to-define words, even for Buddhists. It is often described as being fully awake — directly perceiving the nature of self and reality. Another approach holds that the distinction between knower and what is known dissolves.

Buddha left a collection of teachings about life and death called the *dharma*. He spoke about ways to end suffering that comes with all human existence and how to attain freedom from future incarnations. All of this hinged on the concept of *impermanence*. Everything in the material world is in the process of constant dissolving, constant becoming. The sun comes and goes every day. The moon waxes and wanes. So it is with being born and dying. To understand that everything is transitory is the first step toward freeing oneself from both desire and attachment.

In the Buddhist tradition, there is no concept of "soul," as in other traditions. There is only a "stream of consciousness" that drops its personality like a set of worn-out clothes, and moves on to another incarnation. Dissolving, becoming. As with the other wisdom traditions, Buddhism has many variations, depending on when and where the seed of the teachings happened to fall.

Tibetan Buddhism

There's a well-known tale of impermanence that arose when the Dalai Lama was coming to visit San Francisco in 1981. A group of Tibetan monks created a sand mandala at the Asian Art Museum in his honor. Colored crystals of sand were used in an intricate design in a large space on the floor. For some unknown reason after it was completed, a woman who was viewing the design jumped on it and started kicking the sand in all directions, destroying the artwork. The police were called and the woman was arrested. The monks calmly went to work and made another mandala. They said they only had love and compassion for the woman. In keeping with the recognition of impermanence, they destroyed the sand painting after the Dalia Lama's visit anyway.

In his recent book, *Advice on Dying and Living a Better Life,* the Dalai Lama describes his daily reflection on his own impermanence. "I am habituating myself to the process," he says, "and thus at the actual time of death, these steps will supposedly be familiar. But whether I will succeed or not, I do not know."

As head of his Tibetan Buddhism lineage, he greets death with humility — and understands that no amount of preparation can guarantee how he will react, when that moment comes, or whether he will escape the wheel of reincarnation and return to life another time. One of this tradition's most beautiful stories is how each Dalai Lama is recognized by his people as an incarnation of a previous spiritual leader.

The 13th Dalai Lama had passed away in 1933. After a specified amount of time lapsed, a group of monks began the search for his replacement. They traveled the countryside, looking for children who seemed likely candidates. Among their questions: Does any child exhibit any special knowledge without being taught? Has anyone witnessed any unusual portents? It is said that in the Tibetan city of Lhasa, the people spontaneously began singing about two young parents who had given birth to a boy named Tenzin Gyatso in 1935. This young boy was able to identify the two monks sent to question him. When the monks presented him with six objects, he was able to identify the two that belonged to the previous leader. In 1940, there was a formal ceremony to name Tenzin Gyatso the next Dalai Lama.

Contemporary Stories of Reincarnation

Every so often we hear stories of young children who appear to have "special knowledge" of past lives — and remember events that they could not have possibly learned about through normal means. Jim B. Tucker, an associate psychiatry professor at the University of Virginia Medical Center's Division of Perceptual Studies, has collected more than 2,500 such cases. Tucker put some of the most compelling stories into his book, *Return to Life: Extraordinary Cases of Children Who Remember Past Lives.*

According to Dr. Tucker, one out of five of these children recall the time between death and rebirth, although there is no consistent view of what that time is like. Some allege they were in "God's house," while others claim they waited near their loved ones before "going inside" their new mothers. Dr. Tucker also reported that nearly 20 percent of these children have scar-like birthmarks, deformities or injuries associated with the person whose life the child recalls.

A case in point is the story of Ryan Hammons who lives in Oklahoma. When he was four years old, he informed his mother that he used to be a Hollywood actor. During the night he would shout "Action" as if he were directing a movie. Ryan described a swimming pool at the actor's home in Los Angeles, and said he had three sons. He became very insistent about finding out the names of those sons. He was so insistent, his mother Cyndi went to the library and got some books on Hollywood movies. As she and her son were leafing through a book, they saw a photograph from the 1930s movie, *Night After Night*. Ryan pointed to an actor in a minor role and said: "That guy's me. I found me."

It took months for Cyndi to find the name of the actor because he was not credited in the film. She contacted Dr. Tucker who found a film archivist who was able to identify him. The actor's daughter confirmed many details that Ryan had told Dr. Tucker, including the fact that the actor lied about his age. At a meeting with the actor's daughter, Ryan hid behind his mother and wouldn't talk.

"I think [these children] see that no one is waiting for them in the past," Tucker says. "Some of them get sad about it, but ultimately they accept it and they turn their attention more fully to the present. They get more involved in experiencing this life, which, of course, is what they should do."

The Universal Appeal of Reincarnation

Reincarnation is mentioned many times in the Jewish mystical book known as the *Zohar*. Certain African and Native American tribes believe that we die and return in another body. And even though mainstream Christianity holds that you live only one life, a Pew Forum poll in 2009 found that 24 percent of American Christians expressed a belief in reincarnation.

One of our nation's founding fathers, Benjamin Franklin, predicted he would return. This is the epitaph he wrote for himself:

The Body of B. Franklin, Printer; like the Cover of an old Book, Its Contents torn out, And stript of its Lettering and Gilding, Lies here, Food for Worms. But the Work shall not be wholly lost; For it will, as he believ'd, appear once more, In a new & more perfect Edition, Corrected and amended By the Author.

While Franklin may have said this in jest, he raises an interesting point, also reflected in Buddhist teachings on reincarnation: the positive possibilities. Was Mozart, who started composing music at age three, the next incarnation of a lineage of composers? Was Eleanor Roosevelt the next incarnation in a lineage of crusaders for human rights? What values and talents do you possess that you would like to have another lifetime or more to perfect?

Like the stories of near-death experiences, stories of reincarnation force us to think outside the box. Sometime in the future, each one of us will step out of the physical world. What will we find? The wisdom of Buddhism reminds us that we can prepare for that transition. The process of aging offers glimpses of impermanence — our memories, parts of our bodies start to show signs of it. Mythologist Joseph Campbell used to say that in the latter part of our lives we need to focus on how we are not our bodies. Words cannot capture the experience, but they can point the way.

Death is not extinguishing the light; it is putting out the lamp because dawn has come.

— Rabindranath Tagore, Indian poet;
winner, Nobel Prize in Literature (1913)

The Story of the Circle

Not for me steel coffins
Nor even a pinewood box.
Lay me out in the wilderness
And let me return to Earth.

Tear my flesh, coyote
And I will run with you
Over the plains.
Take my eyes, eagle
And I will soar with you
In the mountains.
Pick my bones clean, little beetles
And I will flow back
Into the lifestream
To think like a mountain and sing like a river.
— Mary de La Valette

Each one of us is made from molecules of Earth and Water, lit by the Fire of the Sun. When we breathe Air, we become alive. When we stop breathing we die, the fire goes out, and all the physical elements of our bodies go on to create other forms. This is Nature's wondrous story of the cycle of death and a form of rebirth. It also underscores a sense of unity with all other beings.

This tradition arose out of close observation of the cycles of life, as in small tribal groups. Since an individual tribe is rooted in its own ecosystem, there are many variations on rituals for death and beliefs about the afterlife. Common to all are the symbols of circle — the rhythm of the seasons, the phases of the moon, the sun appearing and disappearing every day, the cycle of growth and decay.

In the American Northwest today, native people honor the returning of the salmon from the ocean to the creek where they were spawned. The salmon gives its life so that many others can continue theirs. I described this process in an essay titled *Free Range Salmon*:

> The siren song of home calls me back to the same river mouth, the same stream, the same mothering stretch of pebbles. My final act: I turn my body into a shovel, create a new redd, and frenetically dance out my eggs to be fertilized by a hardy partner who has also seen the world. Scraped raw and fatigued by the effort, I die within a day. I offer

up my body, muscled by ocean life and the final upstream swim, to continue the life of my community: bear, eagle, otter and human.

It may be difficult to feel the spiritual depth of this story if you've spent much of your life indoors. The circle story is basic to Native Americans and indigenous peoples all over the world. Oral tradition, language and ritual serve to reinforce the sense that all the forms and beings, including ourselves, are connected to a larger whole, one that is sacred and thus always treated with respect. Physical death comes so that Life may continue. Some Native American and African tribes hold that a person of high moral character joins the spirit world, where he or she can be counted on to help their descendants and provide guidance to the tribe.

An old Lakota Indian once said, "The child is a person who has just come from the Great Mysterious, and I who am an old man am about to return to the Great Mystery. And so in reality we are very close to each other."

Becoming Part of the Whole

Because indigenous people live so embedded in their ecosystem, the flow of life and the ebb of death are always present in their environment. The course of a lifetime, beginning and end, is all seen as circular, and death is as natural as birth. The center of the tribal lands, the center of the home, the center of the person — all the centers correspond to each other. Death in many Native American traditions is the end of a journey toward the center point, the place where the unification is complete.

In a collection of stories titled *Wisdomkeepers*, Frank Davis, a Pawnee Indian elder, describes a dream about this sense of completion. His wife had recently moved on to that center point, and he longed to join her. He said, "Last night I saw my wife. She came in my sleep. I know it was her. She called my name. She was standing on the other side of a wide road. She said she wanted to be with me, but she couldn't get across the road. She said I'd have to be the one to cross the road if I wanted to be with her. She put her hand out. She's calling me. I miss her so, I think I'll be going over soon."

The belief in another dimension of existence has long been a basic tenet of tribal cultures. The words attributed to Chief Seattle of the Duwamish tribe of the Northwest to a gathering of white and native peoples in 1854 served as a warning: "[T]he dead are not powerless. Dead, did I say? There is no death, only a change of worlds."

In the Northern Cheyenne tribe of Montana, it is held that some individuals may travel to the land of the departed and return, with the help of a powerful medicine person. Those individuals can recall visiting those who have died long ago and describe being in a beautiful place. (This is similar to the near-death experience stories described in Chapter 3.) This is why a person who dies is not buried for four days, thus giving an opportunity for return. After that, the Cheyenne believe that the spirit-self moves on to the place of the ancestors, but continues its awareness and participation in the Cheyenne community through dreams and other channels for giving advice such as vision quests. Anthropologist Anne S. Straus states that the Cheyennes believe these spirits "are conscious of the moral order within which they continue to function: they know how to behave in the Cheyenne Way. They are no longer alive and they are no longer human; but they are indeed persons, full participants in the tribal society."

It is good to be reminded that as we move through the seasons of our lives — birth, adolescence, midlife, elderhood, and death — each turn of the Wheel of Life offers opportunities for spiritual awareness, the sense of being one with all else. The turn toward death may offer the clearest opportunity of all. The paradox is revealed:

Death opens us up to Life, as captured in the following Navajo chant:

The mountains, I become part of it...
The herbs, the fir tree, I become part of it.
The morning mists, the clouds, the gathering waters,
I become part of it.
The wilderness, the dew drops, the pollen,
I become part of it.

Hearing this chant during the dying time is comforting to one on the threshold of departure.

Returning to the Earth

When my much-loved 18-year-old cat Snooky died, I put her ashes at the base of a bare root Fuji apple tree I planted in my garden. On the day I saw the first leaves sprouted on a tender-tipped branch, I never felt more connected to the Circle of Life. "She's back," I thought. "We will connect to each other in another way." We seem to know instinctively that our hearts can stay open to the people — and the animal companions — we've loved.

Burial choices sometimes reflect one's choice of story. The great majority of people who die in the US choose either a cemetery burial or cremation. But those choices are changing, due, in part, to a growing environmental consciousness as well as more awareness about the importance of "returning to the earth." Before a close friend died in 2010, she had chosen a "green burial" in the Fernwood Cemetery in Mill Valley, CA. When another dear friend was dying in 2014, he had given instructions to be cremated and his ashes scattered on Lake Michigan where he had spent many joyful summers.

Adjacent to the Golden Gate National Recreation Area, Fernwood is one of the first "green cemeteries" in the country. The burial options include a biodegradable pine box, wicker casket or cloth shroud. No chemicals are used to preserve the bodies. Fernwood describes itself as a consecrated place where "the living and the dead are connected through cycles of nature," and as a safe habitat where native wildlife can raise their young. As of 2015, there were 340 places in forty-one states billed as "green cemeteries." *Recompose* is working on a project to "gently return us to earth after we die." It's taking the next step in the natural burial movement — composting human bodies with a covering of carbon-rich materials like wood chips.

Cremation ashes can be kept by the family, or scattered in the usual ways — on a garden or on a body of water. But today you can also choose to memorialize your loved one in a piece of jewelry or inside a teddy bear. Some of the most imaginative approaches include *Heavenly Stars*, a company that packs cremains into a big-burst fireworks display; *Carbon Copies* can make over 200 pencils from your ashes, with your name emblazoned on each one; and another company says it will take your ashes on trip into outer space on a rocket called *Celestis*.

What we have learned so far is that each tradition or story of death contains elements of dissolution, reconfiguration and transcendence. The Native American tradition captures this multidimensional approach through the dissolution of the body back into elements to be used by others, reconfiguration of the individual into ancestor, and transcendence into the center, where every circle and cycle merge into the changeless. We'll see in the next chapter how an individual can seed the eternal values cultivated in one life into the lives of others.

Legacy Letters

Jon, my dear sweet Jon, I love you beyond words.

I have been delighted time and again by your bright mind and kind heart, by your honesty and humor, by your courage in facing some big challenges. The times of cuddling and playing with you as a child are among my life's sweetest. And we've had a lot of fun along the way — playing games and sports, visiting playgrounds, parks, gardens and beaches, skiing, family reunions, trips to Tuolumne Meadows, cooking together. You've been my closest companion, and you have challenged me and caused me to change in good ways.

Leaving you is the saddest of my thoughts about dying.

I want you to know that I feel I have been blessed with an abundance of joys in my life — in the very experience of being alive; in the beauty of the natural world, the flowers and trees and myriad creatures, the glorious vistas, sunsets, and starry nights; in delight with other people, the love of family, and beloved friends; in the astounding treasury of art, music, literature, and science; in the awesome vastness of the universe, and of the inner world; in the kindness of strangers.

I wish these joys for you also. And one more: Once in a while, please give yourself this gift from me: go to some place in nature and, for a few minutes, just sit, relax, breathe, quiet down, listen, feel, be.

Perhaps my greatest legacy is finding happiness in helping others, in gestures of friendship, in stories told and heard, in the pleasures of food and company and intimacy, in writing and editing, in good projects to help heal the world, in picking up litter, in making music, in creative thinking, and . . . in simply "kissing the moment."

My deepest sorrow is the hurts I have brought to others, and, especially, the times when I lost it with you. I hope you understand that was me stumbling over myself, not any fault of yours; and I am ever thankful for your generous forgiveness. I am grateful for your mom also, for the wonderful mother, guide, and friend she has been.

I must also say that I am anguished by the strife in the world, and by the destruction the global environment has suffered during my lifetime, which will no doubt impact yours. I don't know that I've done the best I could, but I have cared and studied and shouted and tried to help turn things around in the face of the onslaught.

And, you know, I have laughed a lot too.

Jon, stay strong, keep love in your heart, you won't go wrong.

— Dad

At age seventy years and in good health, my friend Shams Kairys wrote this letter to his son. A legacy letter, or ethical will, as it's sometimes called, is a way to share your values and life lessons with those who will live beyond your death. This heartfelt expression of what has truly mattered in your life can be a priceless gift.

Here's another legacy letter, written by my friend Judith Frank to her beloved nieces and nephews:

Dearest Ones,

Cherishing and family go together for us: we're fortunate to hold this precious gift. As our generations unfold we continue to embrace "old country" values we inherited from mothers and fathers who came before us. Family.

I sit on the sidelines, having no children of my own. While my attention was necessarily on my own life, my loving eyes were always on you. Witnessing your physical, emotional, intellectual and creative growth over the years has been one of the great joys of my life. My relationship with each of you is distinct from the others, but every one of them is for me its own expression of our family cherishing. Without that, without you, the meaning of my life would have been profoundly diminished. Thank you.

My wish for you is to continue the loving you share today and to pass it gently on to family members who follow.

— Aunt Judy

Imagine reading these words from an ancestor you never met. Someone who took the time to describe what she values and pass her wisdom on to you. How grateful would you be that she did that?

Here is another legacy letter written by a grandmother:

Dear Grandsons,

I am writing to you because there are some important things I want you to know. Although I very much hope to live a long life, to watch you grow up, and to share many thoughts, feelings and adventures along the way, one usually does not know when they will have their turn at dying.

I love you each dearly. You are so lucky to have each other. I hope you always stay close in heart. You are very different and can learn a lot from each other and enjoy new things with each other. Be curious and check out new ways of thinking and looking at life. Wonder about your relationships, your self, your place in the world, and the universe. Admire people you respect and love. Be useful to your family, your community and the world. Develop your talents and offer them for the benefit of all.

Most of all, trust yourself, and love what is good and beautiful. Love freely, fully and well. You are two wonderful, remarkable human beings. You are blessed with healthy bodies, bright minds and tender hearts. You are brave and strong-hearted. Go forth and live well. I love you.

— Amma

Barack Obama wrote a legacy letter to his two daughters, Malia and Sasha, on January 18, 2009, two days before his inauguration as President of the United States. Here is an excerpt:

When I was a young man, I thought life was all about me — about how I'd make my way in the world, become successful, and get the things I want. But then the two of you came into my world with all your curiosity and mischief and those smiles that never fail to fill my heart and light up my day. And suddenly, all my big plans for myself didn't seem so important anymore. I soon found that the greatest joy in my life was the joy I saw in yours. And I realized that my own life wouldn't count for much unless I was able to ensure that you had every opportunity for happiness and fulfillment in yours. In the end, girls, that's why I ran for President: because of what I want for you and for every child in this nation.

In his book *Return to Character*, New York Times columnist David Brooks observes, "Many of us are clearer on how to build an external career than how to build inner character." He describes the difference between "resume virtues and eulogy virtues." Resume virtues are about awards and achievements. Eulogy virtues are about the values that you leave behind. Similarly, a legacy letter is not about accolades. It's about what inspired a person to create a fulfilling life.

Here's an excerpt from a "words of wisdom" letter that a grandmother gave to her children and grandchildren. She reminds us that legacy letters don't have to be solemn or sad.

> Everything changes: just because the baby is throwing her pacifier out of her crib today does not mean she will do so forever.
>
> When you are thinking a lot about a friend who is sick, send them a note, email, or text. All you need to say is Thinking of You, and you will make their day.
>
> Don't leave the toilet paper roller empty.
>
> Give good long hugs to those you love.

Keep flowers in the house. Keep prunes in the house after a certain age.

Dance your ass off.

When you love someone, tell them, don't wait for them to say it.

Be true to your values always. If you let yourself down, make reparations.

Be grateful every night and every morning for what you have.

Make Kindness your religion.

In an essay on "Jewish Views and Customs on Death," Ellen Levine, former director of psychosocial oncology research at the University of California in San Francisco, wrote, "According to Jewish tradition, our lives are measured by our deeds and by whether we have lived up to our full potential. Therefore, the time before death is usually spent in a review of one's life." She says that the questions to be pondered are: Did I do all I could have done to make this world a better place? Was I helpful to others? Author Viktor Frankl captures this in a stark way: "We who lived in the concentration camps can remember those who walked through the huts comforting others, giving away their last piece of bread...."

An ethical will, or legacy letter, is a summary of the values a person wishes to pass down to later generations. Clergy and spiritual counselors often use ethical wills to help focus a person facing death feel a sense of connection and continuity. One sentiment commonly expressed in this document is: Walk in the world for me. Do as I would do, at my best moments. In his book, *After One-Hundred-And-Twenty*, author Hillel Halkin points out that in the ethical will "the silenced voice of the dead is restored, but it does not speak to the mourner. It addresses the post-mourner who is fully back to the difficult business of living."

Another form of the legacy letter is your epitaph. We heard earlier from Ben Franklin who compared himself to a well-worn book. Stan Laurel, of Laurel and Hardy fame, described his contribution — and came up with the wording of his epitaph — on his deathbed:

A master of comedy, his genius in the art of humor brought gladness to the world he loved.

In *Your Legacy Matters*, Rachael Freed reminds us, "None of us knows when our time is up. I am writing to remind you of your love for the people in your life: your spouse or partner, your children and grandchildren, your extended families, your work colleagues, and your friends. I am writing to urge you to take time *now* to express that love. Tomorrow may be too late! While you have time, awareness, and access to your mind and heart, write a legacy letter telling your people of your love for them, what matters in your relationship with them, and what matters most to you in this world."

Love, Strength in Family, Kindness, Good Deeds — these are the legacy values that are universally recognized as the ground for the next generation to stand on. As we'll see in the next chapter, even those who choose to end their own lives can leave behind a positive testimonial that expresses their love to their descendants.

~

The Summoning of Everyman is a 16th-century play still being performed today. It opens with the Angel of Death visiting Everyman, telling him his time on earth is up and he must die. Everyman asks for a brief respite, hoping to find someone to accompany him on that journey. The angel agrees. First Everyman asks a friend to accompany him, but the man is busy. Next Everyman goes to his relatives, who also refuse to join him in death.

Frustrated, Everyman then turns to Worldly Goods, Beauty, Strength and Knowledge. One by one, they explain why they cannot follow him into the next realm. Only Good Deeds is available and is willing to accompany Everyman on his journey. After a soul-searching confession of his misdeeds, Everyman is ready to follow the Angel of Death. At the end of the play, a doctor addresses the audience and drives the moral home:

> Listen all, both old and young. Forsake your pride for it will deceive you in the end. Remember what you have seen: Beauty, Wits, Strength and Discretion, all abandoned Everyman in the end. Only his Good-Deeds went with him to his reckoning.

Like Everyman, when Death knocks on my door, I may look for someone to accompany me. My husband and I are deeply bonded and he might make the offer. I would tell him: "Live for the both of us — keep doing those Good Deeds. I'll see you when you get here."

Stories of Self-Deliverance

August 18, 2014 — *I will take my life today around noon. It is time. Dementia is taking its toll and I have nearly lost myself. I have nearly lost me. Jonathan, the straightest and brightest of men, will be at my side as a loving witness.*

I have known that I have dementia, a progressive loss of memory and judgment, for three years. It is a … "silent disease," one that can lurk for years or even decades before its symptoms become obvious. Ever so gradually at first, much faster now, I am turning into a vegetable. I find it hard to keep in my mind that my granddaughter is coming in three days' time and not today. I have constantly to monitor what I say in an attempt not to make some gross error of judgment.

There comes a time, in the progress of dementia, when one is no longer competent to guide one's own affairs. I want out before the day when I can no longer assess my situation, or take action to bring my life to an end.… Understand that I am giving up nothing that I want by committing suicide. All I lose is an indefinite number of years of being a vegetable in a hospital setting, eating up the country's money but having not the faintest idea of who I am…. I have done my homework. I have reviewed my options. [One is to] end my own life by taking adequate barbiturates to do the job before my mind has totally gone. Ethically, this seems to me the right thing to do….

Today, now, I go cheerfully and so thankfully into that good night. Jonathan, the courageous, the faithful, the true and the gentle, surrounds me with company. I need no more. It is almost noon.

On a Monday in August, 2014, eighty-five-year-old Gillian Bennett took her mattress outdoors so she could look at the mountains near her home on Bowen Island in Canada. She had a good-sized shot of whiskey and a glass of water laced with the narcotic Nembutal. Perhaps her death helped persuade the Canadian government to revisit its stance against self-deliverance. In February, 2015, the Supreme Court of Canada ruled that prohibiting medical aid-in-dying violated the constitutional rights of people who are suffering intolerably. The Canadian legislature then began working on the language of a law that would meet that directive.

Suicide

Many people, including thousands of military veterans and teenagers, commit suicide each year. If you believe that suicide is morally wrong, then this chapter is not for you. But first let me be clear: I am not advocating suicide. I am considering the story of self-deliverance, which is an umbrella term. It includes a variety of legally distinct terms such as "medical aid-in-dying" and "death with dignity," where the dying person controls the process from beginning to end. Western societies have long held the Judeo-Christian commandment of *Thou shalt not kill* to include oneself. Eastern societies are more accepting of the taking of one's own life for a variety of reasons — having to do with honor or political protest.

As Gillian Bennett decided, there are circumstances under which someone might choose to "die with dignity" rather than spend "years being a vegetable." These include enduring intolerable pain and suffering or being so drugged that there is no quality of life. As medical science has discovered more ways to prolong a life, without insuring its quality, this particular form of suicide has been on the rise. Taking one's own life after a diagnosis of terminal illness, or Alzheimer's disease, has now risen to the level of an international issue. Belgium, the Netherlands, Switzerland and Germany permit some form of euthanasia.

In March of 2015, a large majority of the French Parliament voted to allow terminally ill patients with hours or days left to cease treatment and receive continuous palliative sedation until they die. Under law, they can now request general anesthesia that will put them into a state of deep sleep until they die of dehydration, or the underlying disease. Palliative sedation differs from euthanasia in that no one decides the time of death. A poll showed 96 percent of French citizens in favor of this legislation.

The Right-to-Die Movement

In the US, several states have followed the lead of Oregon. In 1997, it was the first state to allow mentally capable, terminally ill adults diagnosed with six months or fewer to live the option to obtain a doctor's prescription for life-ending medication. The person can then decide when to take it and thereby peacefully end unbearable suffering and die in their sleep. Interestingly, nineteen years after Oregon allowed this option, fewer than 2,000 people made this choice. Concerns about hasty decisions, or families pushing for access to an inheritance, seem unfounded. The California legislature allowed its residents the right to medical aid-in-dying in the fall of 2015, and the bill was later signed into law by Governor Jerry Brown. As of this writing, "right-to-die" laws are being debated in over two dozen state legislatures.

Having the right to choose death has sparked a national debate. Between the groups who strongly oppose self-deliverance and those who feel it's an absolute right lies a huge gray area of uncertainty. This chapter provides food for thought and suggestions for further exploration. Here is a statement from one person who is strongly in favor of the right to choose one's own death:

As a hospice volunteer married to a Holocaust survivor I am no stranger to death and dying. I can say this: the right to NOT be forced to go on living, to be given the choice to die a swift, painless death by injection or ingestion...at the patient's/person's request...is a basic human right that you or I cannot deny another person. Aid in dying, which the Canadian Supreme Court has recently said must be the law of its land, means that medical personnel no longer must play or get to play God. It is the patient who is the supreme decider. The right to die is a basic human right. Neither you or anyone else can deny me that right.

In May 2015, Sandra Bem, a Cornell University psychology professor, was featured on the cover of the *New York Times* magazine. After five years of coping with Alzheimer's disease, she self-delivered with the help of the narcotic pentobarbital. Bem had carefully documented her experience from diagnosis to choosing the day to die. As her disease progressed, she began telling those closest to her that she planned to end her life. She typed in her journal: "What I want is to die on my own timetable and in my own nonviolent way."

Bem was adamant that she would take her life when she no longer could articulate coherent sentences. As that began to happen, other priorities took center stage. She experienced the joy of holding her first grandchild and reading picture books. When Bem couldn't identify a lion or a zebra, she'd say, "Oh, it's some animal." By the time she reached her target date of May 20, 2014, she could no longer identify her daughter or write in her journal. Bem poured herself a glass of wine and mixed her own narcotic cocktail, and died within an hour.

During the worst of the AIDS epidemic in San Francisco in the 1980s, people held "self-deliverance" parties to celebrate their lives before that ugly disease took them to their deaths. Those seriously afflicted were often in their twenties or thirties. A few days or weeks later, word came that an "angel" — usually a nurse familiar with narcotics — had helped them make their desired transition.

The man known as the "Father of the Oregon Death with Dignity Act," Dr. Peter Goodwin, took advantage of the law himself at the age of eighty-three. He had practiced as a physician in Oregon for over thirty years, championed the law in the 1990s, and then helped to found the organization Compassion & Choices where he served as its first national medical director. In 2011, he was diagnosed with a rare brain disease. In an interview with Compassion & Choices he said:

Now I have a terminal illness, an unusual brain disease. It's called corticobasal degeneration. What it does, it's inexorably forward marching, and there is no treatment for it. So I've basically lost the function in my right hand, and I have a tremendous tremor in it as well. And my left hand is becoming more and more affected. My legs are becoming more and more affected. So I have difficulty walking, and more and more difficulty at times knowing where my right arm is. I hardly ever know where it is, and it does all sorts of things unexpectedly and independently. I'm determined that I'm not going to die the way this disease would force me to die, which is in a vegetative state.

He made his plan known to his four children and his friends.

I've tried to visualize what it will be like. It will be a very, very sorrowful time, and I'm not looking forward to it. But I am glad to be doing it my way, on my terms. One of the most important things I have learned about the experience is that these important end-of-life decisions are at the core of human liberty. I have had to learn to live — and end — my life as a person, not a physician. This is not about lawyers. This is not about physicians. This is not about politics. This is about real people. People facing the end of their lives with dignity. I am glad to be a part of that legacy.

On March 11, 2012, Peter Goodwin utilized medical aid-in-dying to peacefully end his suffering. He followed the process described in the right-to-die legislation he helped to pass.

Counseling Options

While legislators and voters sort out what's legal or moral about medical aid-in-dying, people are suffering without access to — or knowledge of — the full range of end-of-care options. The organization Compassion & Choices tries to fill the void by offering free phone consultations and support to educate terminally ill adults about all their end-of-life care options, including hospice and palliative care. Compassion & Choices opposes euthanasia, which is illegal throughout the U.S., because someone other than the terminally ill adult administers the medication. In contrast, medical aid-in-dying laws require terminally ill adult to self-ingest the medication, so they can decide if — and when — to take the medication, or not. The organization points out that the decision is highly individual. Here is a testimonial from their website:

> I want to thank you for the wonderful support you gave me when my despair was the greatest, when

I knew I had stage two sarcoma in my thigh and was certain that the cancer had metastasized to my chest. Well, I was completely wrong, and the sarcoma was successfully removed. I just want to tell you that you kept me from doing something so dreadful that it is very hard to say how grateful I am for your organization and people like you....

Among other organizations offering active listening and legal advice is Final Exit Network, based in Tallahassee, Florida. This mission statement can be found on its website:

Our services are free and are offered to our members in all fifty states. Our guides travel to you and educate you on your personal choices. You must, however, be able to competently choose, as well as be able to effect your exit. We believe no one should suffer a traumatic death, and we will do our best — within the limits of each state's laws — to educate you on your alternatives.

Another right-to-die organization based in Scotland, Exit Euthanasia, was founded in 1980 with the purpose of researching and making available reliable information on how to end one's life if faced with unbearable and unrelievable suffering. Their website and blog provide the latest on what they call "the best academic knowledge in the field" of self-deliverance. A book by Chris Docker, *Five Last Acts*, offers step-by-step instructions on how to end your life.

The "acts" include: the use of helium, compression of the carotid arteries, the use of narcotic drugs, the use of sedatives and a plastic bag, and fasting. Each of these methods requires preparation beforehand. Docker advises people to pursue all palliative care alternatives before turning to suicide.

Exit emphasizes that "being at ease with oneself, one's loved ones and the rest of the world is just as much a part of a 'good death' as is lack of pain and indignity in the final moments."

What About Those Left Behind?

A suicide encountered by an unsuspecting family and friends can be a huge emotional assault. I remember being in a large auditorium in San Francisco when Buddhist teacher Jack Kornfield was asked this question: "My closest friend just committed suicide and I'm devastated. What can I do?" Instead of answering directly,

Kornfield turned to the audience: "Who in here has also been touched by a devastating suicide?" I saw that at least twenty percent of the audience raised their hands. Kornfield said to the questioner: "Look around and see how many people share your pain." We were all deeply moved.

In *Knocking on Heaven's Door,* Katy Butler tells how she shepherded each of her parents through the end of their lives. Her role was made much more difficult by what she calls an explosion of life-support technologies that have created an "epidemic of unnecessary death-bed suffering." Butler supports freedom of choice about death, but says what's more important are "brave, truthful doctors willing to discuss when to stop fighting for maximum longevity and explore, instead, what may matter more to us."

What matters more, in Butler's view, is the quality of the last days with a loved one who's dying. "Witnessing death in an intensive care unit often leaves family members with depression, anxiety, and complicated grief. So does taking one's life without saying goodbye."

The Dalai Lama also cautions that "by taking a pill or an injection to have a so-called peaceful death you may be depriving yourself of a crucial opportunity for manifesting virtue." In other words, suffering itself may have something to teach us.

~

Shakespeare's Hamlet has remained one of the most enduring figures in English literature, perhaps because he dared to contemplate his own death:

To be, or not to be, that is the question:
Whether 'tis Nobler in the mind to suffer
The Slings and Arrows of outrageous Fortune,
Or to take Arms against a Sea of troubles,
And by opposing end them: to die, to sleep
No more; and by a sleep, to say we end
The Heart-ache, and the thousand Natural shocks
That Flesh is heir to? 'Tis a consummation
Devoutly to be wished....

Tapestry:
Brief Stories of Completion

Just as when weaving
One reaches the end
With fine threads woven throughout;
So is the life of humans.
— Buddha

While stories can offer comfort during the dying time, all you may need is a brief poem, or an image, or even just a few words. This chapter contains inspiring lines from writers, poets and spiritual teachers offering guidance on crossing the threshold. Perhaps one of these will be sufficient.

Sea turns on itself and foams:
With every foaming bit
another body, another being takes form.
And when the sea sends word,
each foaming body
melts immediately back to ocean-breath.

— Rumi
as translated by Neil Douglas-Klotz,
scholar of ancient Middle Eastern languages

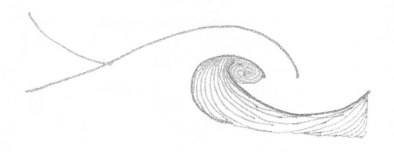

Because I could not stop for Death —
He kindly stopped for me —

— Emily Dickinson, poet (1830-1886)

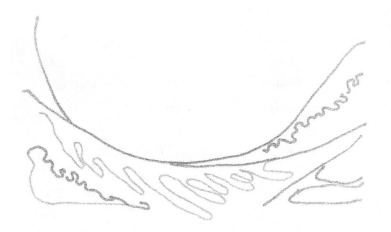

Death is your best friend.
When you can endure life no longer,
death comes and sets you free.

— Mark Twain

Who we think we are dies, but we are not
who we think we are.

— Anonymous

Don't be afraid. Someone who loves you
is waiting with open arms.

— based on thousands of hospice reports of dying people
seeing escorts waiting for them

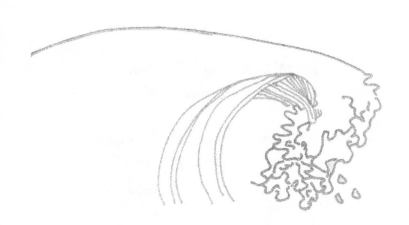

I lie down this night with God
And God will lie down with me.

— from *Celtic Visions* by Esther de Waal

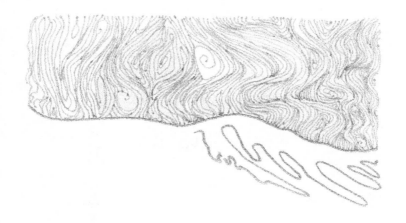

From Light have you come, to light shall you go,
and surrounding you
through every step is the light of your
infinite being.

— Richard Bach, author of *Jonathan Livingston Seagull*

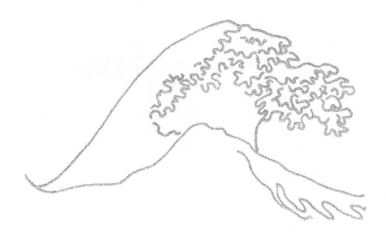

I'm off to my next great adventure.

— Spoken by Willis Harman on his deathbed.
Harman was a professor at Stanford University,
and head of the Institute of Noetic Sciences,
founded by astronaut Edgar Mitchell.

A little while, a moment of rest upon the wind,
and another woman shall bear me.

— from *The Prophet,* by Kahlil Gibran

*I do believe I've completed the main body
of what I signed up for. There's always more
that could be done, but I feel I've done enough.*

— Rabbi Zalman Schachter-Shalomi
Founder of the Jewish Renewal Movement

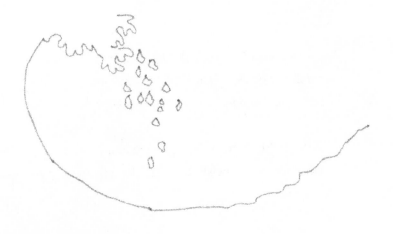

The four things that matter most to say
during your dying time:

Please forgive me.

I forgive you.

Thank you.

I love you.

— *The Four Things That Matter Most,* by Ira Byock, M.D.,
internationally recognized palliative-care physician

The Lord is my shepherd; I shall not want…
Yea, though I walk through the valley of the shadow of death,
I will fear no evil: for thou art with me…
I will dwell in the house of the Lord forever.

— From Psalm 23 (KJV)

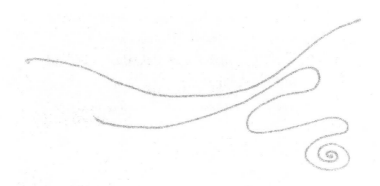

You are a drop returning to the embrace of
Mother Ocean

Welcome to the Beloved Community

You are leaving the world of suffering.
Welcome to the Divine Light

You are returning to the Center of the Circle

The pain of separation is over. You are dissolving
into the Ground of All Being

— Messages from the Wisdom Traditions

The Story of Transformation

*"I've seen a seven-foot all-white Angel stand-
ing in the hallway a couple of times this week.
I think the Angel is here to take me home."*

I was in conversation with my friend of forty years the
week before he died of lung disease. He told me that
the angel had been as present as I was that day. We
were sitting in his office and I could see the computer
screen over his shoulder. Emails were pouring in from
his friends, sending him love and healing energy.

I asked him if he wanted to talk about dying and
he shook his head no. A few days later, his wife called
me after he died and invited me to spend time with
his body. It had only been a couple of hours. Maybe
his spirit was still present in the room. I asked him if
he had anything to tell me. He had been a jazz musi-
cian all his life. I suddenly looked up at the ceiling and
from a corner I distinctly heard When the Saints
Go Marching In. It sounded like it was coming from
an old time radio. Several months later that was the

theme song at his memorial service attended by hundreds of people.

⁓

My friend's description of his encounter with the Angel was a bit startling. But according to hospice nurses and counselors, seeing otherworldly escorts during the dying time is a common experience. In her book, *The Grace in Dying*, Kathleen Dowling Singh observed that when you have accepted that you are in your dying time, a process of unification begins, and you may begin to experience larger, transpersonal levels of reality.

> In the dying process, people experience transformation in the movement from tragedy to grace. Grace is the experience of finally, gratefully, relaxing the contraction of fearful separation and opening to Spirit as our own radiant splendor: knowing it, feeling it, entering it, as it enters us.

In her decades of work with hospice patients, Dr. Singh concluded that for some people this process can begin several months or weeks prior to the death of the body; for others it may begin hours or even minutes before the final surrender. For others, it seems not to happen at all. During the dying time, spiritual beliefs can reawaken, even if they've been lying dormant for years. It's also possible to have your first true spiritual experience in this transition period.

In this chapter, we'll examine the Story of Transformation, which can be found in many of the wisdom traditions — that moment when the drop starts falling back into the wave and begins to surrender its individual identity. Transformation in death has a spectrum of meanings, depending on the source. It can mean surrender, an acceptance of the fact that my life in this body is ending. It can mean a larger awareness of the impermanence of everything, as Buddhism suggests. It can mean a complete dissolution into the Ground of All Being, as writer Aldous Huxley highlights in so many ways in *The Perennial Philosophy*. Author Richard Bach captures a version in his well-known quote: "What the caterpillar calls the end of the world, the master calls a butterfly."

People have made many attempts to grasp the dimension of union with the Divine in a word or two. They include personal names, such as Allah or Jesus, or impersonal words like Light, Love, Spirit, or the Source. The Chinese Taoist text, the Tao Te Ching, puts it best in its opening line: *The Tao that can be spoken is not the eternal*

Tao. What those names point to is essentially unnamable, ineffable, beyond words.

As in the story above, the dying/transforming person sometimes sees figures that are invisible to everyone else. Most often the person describes loved ones who have already passed away, and talks with them as if they were present and alive. My father saw his deceased wife Rita standing at the foot of his bed. I was in the room and did not see her. Charles Garfield recounted the story, in the Foreword of this book, of his mother seeing her long-dead mother and father present in the room. Such reports of visits by deceased loved ones, or religious figures, or angels occur across all cultures around the world.

Hazrat Inayat Khan, a Sufi mystic who lived into the early 20th century, suggests that all such visits are from angels in a heavenly realm and that humans can have contact with angels at the time of death. "Many have seen in their lives the angels of death, yet when death's call comes some have seen them in human form. Others have not seen them but heard them speak.... The reason is that a person who has lived on the earthly plane has to clothe a being of the higher planes in earthly garments, and to interpret the language of the higher spheres in his own words."

Here we have another aspect of Mystery, similar to the near-death experience. Are these visits "real" or are they "all in the head"? Perhaps it is a sign of the transformation process, perhaps a glimpse of the persistence of the personality after death. Whether an individual personality lives on, or is extinguished in ineffable Oneness, is part of the Mystery. The wisdom traditions presented in this book emphasize one or both possibilities.

Glimpsing Other Dimensions

Throughout this book, wisdom stories have suggested that there are other dimensions of reality beyond the world we know. How long have human beings been sensing the existence of a transcendent reality? Going back ten thousand to twelve thousand years ago, there is plenty of evidence of belief in a larger dimension. If you were a stranger traveling in the Middle East, you would come upon settlements of humans living in ordinary houses or huts, around a larger empty dwelling in the center. You might think this was the house of the tribal ruler, and you might be right. But in many cases, you would not be able to find an inhabitant, or determine what function this building might have, such as a granary or barn for animals. Adding to the mystery would be the presence of a large table inside, often covered with offerings. Humans still hold that invisible forces are honored in this kind of building. Consider the thousands of temples, churches, ashrams, mosques and synagogues that fill the earth today. Such a place is sometimes referred to as the House of God.

The view that there is more to life than our space/time dimension is elaborated in the teachings of the Buddha (circa 500 BCE), who said that the goal of a lifetime is *nirvana*, a transcending of the boundaries of the finite self. Buddha affirmed the Hindu notion of reincarnation where a person is held on the wheel of *karma*, an accounting of debit and credit entries from the current and past lifetimes. One's account is closed when all debits are cleared. Then one experiences enlightenment, the realization that there is no separate identity, no separate self, because all is flux, all is change, all is impermanent. One can then enter nirvana, a state of bliss — eternal and incomprehensible peace.

A similar story comes from the writings of Joseph Epes Brown, who spent decades in the mid-20th century living with and interviewing North American Indian elders. Brown summarizes the essential Indian experience of life and death in three stages. The first is *purification* of the individual self over a lifetime through prayer, ritual, and carrying out daily activities with a sense of their sacredness. The second stage he calls *perfection*, by which an individual works toward the realization that he or she is not a separate fragment, but contains the whole Universe within. This may come in the form of a dream or a vision where the individual experiences a larger reality beyond the immediate world. Brown describes the third stage as a *state of unity* with the changeless and timeless, a return to Origin, found at the center of every circle. He says the masculine energies of purification and perfection find their rest in a feminine circle of completeness. Death fulfills the union.

Death Is Death

This book has not been an attempt to take the grief, loss, or tragedy out of the dying time. It is an attempt to add an element — a story — that can help make that transition less fearful, less traumatic, and thereby more of a rite of passage. Dr. Singh cautioned that we need, above all, to honor the tragic aspect of dying:

> We are multidimensional beings and, at the level of our pain, the illuminations of a more expanded level are no comfort whatsoever. We comfort each other by meeting each other where we are in the

present moment. The present moment of hearing one's prognosis is a moment of deep suffering, at whatever degree of closeness or distance the pain or the affect of fear may be held from the psyche. Such suffering demands true compassion.... In short, what ensues, from the moment one hears a terminal diagnosis to the moment one surrenders into it, is suffering — the very essence of tragedy.

This is the time of "wrestling with the Angel of Death," when denial of death is more psychologically comforting than acceptance. Dr. Singh called the move toward acceptance "the path of return." She offered the possibility that there is a "fundamental intuition" that begins to dissolve the terrifying sense of the difference between life and death. This is when a person realizes there is a larger dimension of reality where "we move beyond our human sense of history, our past, our fleeting present and our future, into pure Being...."

There's a simple lesson we can take from the story of transformation: that we all have the potential to move away from living from fear toward living from love, *before* we are in our dying time. We can swim in that Ocean of

Love in this lifetime. Simply stated: Live from Love, not from Fear.

It is good to be reminded that this form of transformation, becoming One with All That Is, is possible while we are alive, while we are breathing the air, drinking the waters, and sharing Life with many others. Whether or not we're aware of it, we are participating in an Ocean of Oneness, as we participate in life on planet Earth. Chief Dan George of the Salish tribe of British Columbia suggests ways to cherish it:

> *The beauty of the trees,*
> *the softness of the air,*
> *the fragrance of the grass,*
> *speaks to me.*
> *The summit of the mountain,*
> *the thunder of the sky,*
> *the rhythm of the sea,*
> *speaks to me.*
> *The faintness of the stars,*
> *the freshness of the morning,*
> *the dewdrop on the flower,*
> *speaks to me.*
> *The strength of fire,*

the taste of salmon, the trail of the sun,
and the life that never goes away,
they speak to me.
And my heart soars.

Epilogue

When the world was still young, Truth walked around as naked as she was the day she was born. Whenever she came close to a village, people closed their doors and shut their windows, for everyone was afraid to face the Naked Truth. Understandably Truth felt very alone and lonesome. One day she encountered Story who was surrounded by a flock of people of all ages who followed her everywhere she went. Truth asked her, "Why is it that people love you, but shy away from me?" Story, who was dressed in beautiful robes, advised Truth: "People love colorful clothes. I will lend you some of my robes and you will see that people will love you too." Truth followed her advice and dressed herself in the colorful robes of Story. It is said that from this day on, Truth and Story always walk together and that people love both of them.

In the Introduction, I posed two questions: What happens when we die? What happens after we die?

Another way of asking the second question: Is there personal survival and continuity of soul after what we call death?

As the Yiddish folktale above advises us, when Naked Truth is too frightening, or not available, all we have are stories for answers. Stories can bypass the rational mind by speaking to us in images and metaphors, like the wave and the drop. They can transport us into realms where we share universal symbols beyond language, like heaven or nirvana. Stories remind us that the Cycle of Life and Death is so much larger than an individual existence, or even an individual religion. Stories from the world's religions contain such universals. That is why any one of us can embrace a story originating in a culture not our own. We don't need to take on a religion's doctrines or trappings, the colors and design of the robes, if we don't care to. The stories are drawn from wisdom traditions that have been honed over centuries by the best thinkers and practitioners within the tradition. The stories are treasures for all of us to share with each other.

Another way to hold all these stories is by recalling the wisdom tale of the blind men and the elephant. There's a parable told in the Hindu and Buddhist traditions about a group of four blind men who were each asked by the king to describe an elephant. The men were positioned around the elephant and were asked to describe what they felt. "The elephant is much like a tree," said one. "Yes, it's very much like a tree trunk."

"No, you are quite wrong," said another. "The elephant is much like a piece of heavy cord, rubbery and tough."

A third said, "What I'm feeling is much like a large butterfly. I have a huge, soft piece of something that must be his wing."

The fourth man said, "I have a piece of the creature that is neither like a cord, or a tree, or a butterfly. I think the elephant is much like a python, a thick creature that writhes like a snake."

Then the king explains: "All of you are right. The reason every one of you is telling it differently is because each one of you touched a different part of the elephant. So, actually the elephant has all the features you mentioned."

Maybe the answers to our questions about other realms of existence are contained in the sum of the stories. Maybe each story contains a piece of truth dressed in beautiful robes. Maybe the answer is something we cannot possibly grasp with our finite minds because it's just too big or beyond our ability to comprehend. The mystics of all religions say that each one of us is capable of entering the Mystery. We need only to break through the barrier of finite mind — the part of us that needs to understand, the part of us that resides in the dimensions of time and space. This quote from Zen Buddhism captures how the One Reality contains within itself all realities:

The one Moon reflects itself wherever there is a sheet of water,

And all the moons in the waters are embraced within the one Moon.

One pathway is clear: we create afterlife stories to cope with the grief of losing a loved one. A beloved is in our life one day, and gone the next. In the mornings afterward, we wake up asking, pleading, "Where are you? Where did you go?" We ache to connect with the place where the beloved is now. Maybe our story creates a bridge to that dear one in order to make it so.

Those who study near-death experiences and mediums who say they contact "people on the other side" tell us that the story we hold as we pass through the threshold is the experience we will have upon entry into the afterlife. They also say loved ones who have gone before us are waiting for us, and that our expectations will shape our experiences after we die.

I've learned through writing this book that death is a process, not an event. I've come to appreciate that if one is fortunate enough to have a dying time with loved ones nearby and palliative care, it can be an opening to a greater depth of gratitude for the life one was given. Acceptance of one's death, even when immersed in sadness, can also bring a form of enlightenment not reserved for the saintly. As the boundary between self and other, between the drop and the wave dissolves, we may finally "get it" that the Ocean of Love is all there is. Love is universal and expresses itself in so many ways — friendship, kindness, concern, caring, forgiveness, compassion, courage, commitment to beauty, embracing, grieving, singing....

I began this book because I witnessed firsthand how important it is to have a story about death and afterlife to ride out on. The deaths of my parents and other beloved people in my life showed me that there are a variety of stories to choose from that fill that need. My overall message remains the same: sometimes you need a story more than food, especially during your dying time. Of course, a story isn't all a person needs. We need love, gratitude, care, and a sense that our legacy matters. And to die within a state of grace is a gift beyond measure.

The Story which serves me best is one that steadies the boat so that I can move into acceptance of my mortality — before the wind hits the sails and I head off into the Mystery.

> In learning to sail you do not change the current of the water nor do you have any effect on the wind, but you learn to hoist your sail and turn it this way and that to utilize the greater forces which surround you. By understanding them, you become one with them....
>
> — Author and psychotherapist June Singer

If I can drop back into the Ocean of Love that I've discovered during my dying time, maybe only days or minutes before…that is a mystery as profound as the moment I was born. It is then that I can transcend the boundaries of my small self, and reconvene in the One.

May it be so.

Questions to Consider...

If you have a wisdom story about death or afterlife, does it sustain you in times of grief? Can you draw strength from it?

Which songs would you choose to hear during your dying time?

Do you think that each of us lives many lifetimes?

What values and talents do you possess that you would like to have another lifetime or two to perfect?

Who in your family would appreciate a legacy letter from you?

Which of the people who have died before you would you like as an escort across the threshold?

Do you have a story for your dying time that will help you cross that threshold?

What happens *when* we die?

What happens *after* we die?

Chapter Endnotes and Resources

[For full book references, see *For Further Reading*]

Introduction

"...certain selections of music" is a reference to the work of the Threshold Choir, which has chapters around the United States. Choir members are invited to a dying person's room to sing the person's chosen songs. See also Chapter 2. https://thresholdchoir.org

References to Arnold Toynbee's work all come from his essay, "Man's Concern with Life After Death," from the anthology *Life After Death* (1976). The one cited here is on p. 17.

The World Health Organization (WHO) estimates that approximately 153,000 people die each day, which adds up to 56 million a year.

Ram Dass: Fierce Grace, 2001. DVD distributed by Zeitgeist Films, 2001.

Irvin Yalom, *Staring at the Sun: Overcoming the Terror of Death* (San Francisco: Jossey Bass, 2009), p. 5.

References to Kathleen Dowling Singh's work come from *The Grace in Dying: A Message of Hope, Comfort, and Spiritual Transformation* (San Francisco: Harper One, 2000). This one is on p. 272.

Welsh poet Dylan Thomas (1914–1953) wrote those lines as a refrain in a poem he published in *In Country Sleep, and Other Poems* (New York: New Directions, 1952).

Chapter 1 — The Story of The Wave and The Drop

Huston Smith, *The Illustrated World's Religions: A Guide to Our Wisdom Traditions* (San Francisco: Harper One, 1995), pp. 17-57.

Parables of Rama by Rama Tirtha, Parable 118. See: https://archive.org/details/ParablesOfRamaBySwamiRamaTirtha Not available in print.

You are not a drop... is a line popularly attributed to the Sufi poet Rumi, but scholars argue whether it is his, because it does not appear in classic translations. It captures the sense of the chapter's story, wherever it comes from.

Vibration and form/Heaven and Earth taken from *Desert Wisdom: A Nomad's Guide to Life's Big Questions from the Heart of the Native Middle East* by Neil Douglas-Klotz (2011), pp. 4-5 ARC Press.

Rabbi Zalman Schacter-Shalomi as quoted in *The December Project,* by Sara Davidson (San Francisco: Harper One, 2014), p. 7 and p. 171.

Shema — a Jewish sacred prayer said by a dying person in Hebrew that expresses love of God.

Chapter 2 — The Story of Heaven

Opening story used with permission from Peggy Flynn. She is author of *The Caregiving Zone: A Unique Guide to Facing the Realities of Illness, Aging, Dying and Death* (iUniverse Inc., 2006).

"'The Beloved Community' is a term often associated with Martin Luther King, Jr. At the King Center website, it is explained that the phrase "was first coined in the early days of the 20th century by the philosopher-theologian Josiah Royce, who founded the Fellowship of Reconciliation. However, it was Dr. Martin Luther King, Jr., also a member of the Fellowship of Reconciliation, who popularized the term and invested it with a deeper meaning, which has captured the imagination of people of goodwill all over the world … . Dr. King's Beloved Community is a global vision, in which all people can share in the wealth of the earth. In the Beloved Community, poverty, hunger and homelessness will not be tolerated because international standards of human decency will not allow it." www.thekingcenter.org

Section on Tom Henry came from personal interview. Used with his permission.

Mark Shriver, *Pilgrimage: My Search for the Real Pope Francis* (New York: Random House, 2016). See also an interview with author at https://www.youtube.com/watch?v=anJ_KQV_2Gg

"…*the least of my brethren*…" New Testament, Matthew 25:34 KJV.

Ancient Egypt Heaven cited by Mircea Eliade in his commentary on the *Pyramid Texts* in his *Development of Religion and Thought in Ancient Egypt* (Chicago, 1912).

Quran [41-32]: "We are your friends in this life and in the Hereafter. Therein you will have all that your souls will desire, and therein you will have all that you will ask for."

Swing Low, Sweet Chariot lyrics from www.negrospirituals.com The origin of the song is ambiguous, but it's believed to have been written by a Choctaw freedman in Oklahoma, around 1862.

Howard Thurman (1899-1981): author, philosopher, theologian, educator and civil rights leader. He was Dean of Chapel at Howard University (1932-1944) and at Boston University (1953-1965). This sentiment appears in many of his writings.

Threshold Choir at: https://thresholdchoir.org A six-minute video on the website gives a beautiful summary of their work.

Further insight into bedside singing can be found at www.SoulandMeaning.com, the website of TC member Jan Thomas. There's a link to a twenty-minute video of the singers practicing.

The Pew Research Center, which conducts nationwide surveys on religion, found that in its 2014 survey, 72 percent of all adults "believe in heaven." This cuts across age, income, and educational backgrounds. www.pewforum.org/religious-landscape-study/belief-in-heaven/

Toynbee in *Life After Death,* p. 19.

Chapter 3 — Stories of Near-Death Experiences

Eben Alexander, M.D., *Proof of Heaven: A Neurosurgeon's Journey into the Afterlife* (New York: Simon & Schuster, 2012), p. 38.

Letter from St. Paul taken from New International Version (NIV) of New Testament.

Sheldon Ruderman, "A Personal Encounter with Death and Some Consequences," in the anthology, *Between Life and*

Death, edited by Robert Kastenbaum (New York: Springer Publishing, 1979).

Albert Heim, *Remarks on fatal falls. Yearbook of the Swiss Alpine Club* (1892) 27:327–337. In R. Noyes, Jr. and R. Kletti (trans.). Heim, A. *Omega* (1972) 3:45–52.

CNN program, *Stories of Life, Death, and Faith: To Heaven and Back* aired on November 30, 2013. www.cnn.com

Dr. Mary Neal's story can be found at her website, www.drmaryneal.com. Her book is *To Heaven and Back: A Doctor's Extraordinary Account of Her Death, Heaven, Angels, Her Life Again: A True Story* (Colorado: WaterBrook Press, 2012).

Anita Moorjani has written *Dying to Be Me: My Journey from Cancer, to Near Death to True Healing* (Carlsbad, CA: Hay House, 2014) and *What If This Is Heaven?* (Carlsbad, CA: Hay House, 2016). Her TED talk can be found at https://www.youtube.com/watch?v=rhcJNJbRJ6U.

NDE study 2014 was originally reported in *Resuscitation Journal* (December 2014), pp. 1799-1805. It can also be found under *Near-death Experiences? Results of the world's largest medical study of the human mind and consciousness at the time of death*, University of Southampton (October 7, 2014).

Chapter 4 — The Story of Reincarnation

Laura Huxley's words during Aldous' passing. Laura Huxley, *This Timeless Moment* (New York: Farrar, Straus & Giroux, 1968) p. 305.

Aldous Huxley, quote from *The Perennial Philosophy* (New York: Harper Perennial Modern Classics, 2009), p. viii.

You are dying… . From *The Tibetan Book of the Dead.* Chogyam Trungpa and Francesca Fremantle, *The Tibetan Book of the Dead: The Great Liberation through Hearing in the Bardo* (Boston: Shambhala, 1975), p. 28. Used with permission.

The Dalai Lama and Jeffrey Hopkins, *Advice on Dying and Living a Better Life* (New York: Atria Books, 2002), p. 163.

10-year-old Ryan Hammonds tells of his former life on NBC's Today program on March 16, 2015. www.today.com/video/today/57120459#57120459

More on Ryan in article, "The Science of Reincarnation: University of Virginia Psychiatrist Jim Tucker Investigates Children's Claims of Past Lives" www.uvamagazine.org/articles/the_science_of_reincarnation

Pew Forum poll taken in August, 2009, cited in article, "Many Americans Mix Multiple Faiths." www.pewforum.org/2009/12/09/many-americans-mix-multiple-faiths/

Chapter 5 — The Story of the Circle

Poem by Mary de La Valette, in *Life Prayers from Around the World*, by Elizabeth Roberts and Elias Amidon (San Francisco: HarperSanFrancisco, 1996), p. 327. Used with permission from the poet.

The communion of elements around the changeless center, as described by Joseph Epes Brown in *The Spiritual Legacy of the American Indian* (New York: Crossroads Publishing, 1982), p. 119.

Salmon segment from "Free Range Salmon" by Cindy Spring, article in *EarthLight* magazine (Spring, 2002).

Frank Davis quote taken from *Wisdomkeepers* (Hillsboro, OR: Beyond Words, 1991), p. 101.

Quote from Chief Seattle… . There is a great deal of controversy surrounding Chief Seattle's speech of 1854. There are various versions of the speech, and debates over its very existence. For one documented source, see https://www.archives.gov/publications/prologue/1985/spring/chief-seattle.html.

Story about Northern Cheyenne taken from "The Meaning of Death in Northern Cheyenne Culture," an essay by Anne S. Straus as it appeared in the anthology, *Death, Mourning and Burial: A Cross-Cultural Reader,* edited by Antonius C. G. M. Robben (Blackwell Publishing, 2004), p. 74.

Navajo chant from *I Become Part of It: Sacred Dimensions in Native American Life* (New York: Parabola Books, 2002), p. 20.

Material for "Returning to the Earth" section came from:
Ashes to Ashes, article in *The Huffington Post:*
www.huffingtonpost.com/2014/08/13/cremation-on-the-rise-infographic_n_5669195.html

Ash Scattering: Non-Traditional Ways to Be Memorialized, article in *The Huffington Post:*
www.huffingtonpost.ca/2012/05/25/ash-scattering_n_1545627.html

www.celestis.com for more information on taking ashes to the moon.

Material on natural or green cemeteries can be found at:
www.recompose.life
www.fernwoodcemetery.com

Chapter 6 — Legacy Letters

Letters printed with permission of their writers, through personal communication with the author.

Excerpt of legacy letter written in 2009 from Barack Obama to his daughters, as printed in *Parade Magazine* (August 4, 2013).

"Jewish Views and Customs on Death," by Ellen Levine, essay in *Death and Bereavement Across Cultures,* edited by Colin Murray Parkes, Pittu Laungani, and Bill Young (London: Brunner-Routledge Publishers, 1997).

Viktor E. Frankl, *Man's Search for Meaning* (New York: Washington Square Press, 1988).

Guidance on writing a legacy letter can be found from Rachael Freed's book, *Your Legacy Matters* (Ferndale, MI: Minerva Press, 2013).

Hillel Halkin, *After One-Hundred-And-Twenty: Reflections on Death, Mourning and The Afterlife in The Jewish Tradition* (Princeton, NJ: Princeton University Press, 2016), p. 135.

A good summary of Everyman can be found at www.enotes.com/topics/everyman. The complete script for the play *The Summoning of Everyman* can be found at blanckd.yolasite.

com/resources/Everyman%28Abridged%29.pdf in a modern adapted form.

Chapter 7 — Stories of Self-Deliverance

Complete version of letter from Gillian Bennett can be found at www.deadatnoon.com

Source for story re: French adoption of "deep sleep law": www.theguardian.com/world/2015/mar/17/french-parliament-deep-sleep-law-terminally-ill-euthanasia

Number of medically assisted deaths in Oregon from 1998-2016 published in a State of Oregon report: www.oregon.gov/oha/ph/ProviderPartnerResources/EvaluationResearch/DeathwithDignityAct/Documents/year19.pdf

Source for hospice volunteer, "Offering a Choice to the Terminally Ill" (*New York Times*, March 15, 2015), was an editorial about euthanasia, and it received 227 responses. This respondent's letter was printed in a later edition and she was unnamed.

Sandra Bem's story can be found at "The Last Day of Her Life," *New York Times Magazine*, www.nytimes.com/2015/05/17/magazine/the-last-day-of-her-life.html

More information on *Compassion & Choices*, as well as the Peter Goodwin story can be found at: https://www.compassionandchoices.org/wp-content/uploads/2016/07/Spring_2012_Peter_Goodwin.pdf

Source for Katy Butler: "Aid-in-Dying Laws Are Just a Start," *New York Times Sunday Review* (July 12, 2015), p. 2.

Dalai Lama, *Advice on Dying and Living a Better Life*, p. 105.

Chapter 8 — Tapestry and Other Brief Stories of Completion

Buddha quote taken from *Advice on Dying*, by Dalai Lama, p. 39.

Sea turns on itself... by Rumi, as translated by Neil Douglas-Klotz in *Desert Wisdom*, p. 147, used with permission.

From light have you come... quote from *One, a Novel*, by Richard Bach (New York: Dell Publishing, 1988), p. 150.

Sara Davidson, *The December Project*, p. 70.

Ira Byock, M.D., *The Four Things That Matter Most* (New York: Atria Books, 2004).

Chapter 9 — The Story of Transformation

Opening story: Bud Spangler and I were business partners in an audio production company for 25 years, and deeply close friends for 40 years.

In the dying process..., Kathleen Dowling Singh, *The Grace in Dying*, pp 110-111.

Caterpillar/butterfly quote found in *Illusions: The Adventures of a Reluctant Messiah*, by Richard Bach (New York: Arrow Books, 1977) p. 134.

Hazrat Inayat Khan, as found in *The Sufi Message*, Vol. I (London: Barrie Books Ltd., 1960), p. 119.

The notion of "God's house" in the middle of a village is described as part of the evolution of the God concept in *The Origin of Consciousness in the Breakdown of the Bicameral Mind*, by psychohistorian Julian Jaynes (Boston: Houghton Mifflin Company, 1976), p. 150.

The Transformation Story as told by Joseph Epes Brown, pp. 112-113.

We are multidimensional beings, Kathleen Dowling Singh, pp. 90 and 94.

…we move beyond, found in Kathleen Dowling Singh, pp. 81-82.

"The beauty of the trees," poem by Chief Dan George, as found in Roberts and Amidon, *Earth Prayers from Around the World*, p. 42.

If the Transformation story appeals to you, I highly recommend Kathleen Dowling Singh's *The Grace in Dying*. It expands in detail, with beautiful and sensitive writing, the process she called "The Nearing Death Experience." She crossed that threshold on October 1, 2017. Two days later, her last book, *Unbinding: The Grace Beyond Self*, was published (Somerville, MA: Wisdom Publications, 2017).

Epilogue

Truth and Story taken from "Spiritual Care at the End of Life: How Folktales Can Guide Us," by Christel Lukoff and David Lukoff in *Journal of Transpersonal Psychology* (2011), Vol 43, No 2. Cited from B. Weinreich, *Yiddish Folk Tales* (New York: Schocken, 1988).

Moon quote as found in Aldous Huxley, *The Perennial Philosophy*, p. 8.

The NDE literature contains thousands of stories of visions of afterlife and beloved escorts. For particularly poignant stories, see Lisa Smartt's book (with Raymond Moody), *Words at the Threshold: What We Say as We're Nearing Death* (Novato, CA: New World Library, 2017).

June Singer, *Boundaries of the Soul* (New York: Anchor Books, 1994), p. 13.

For Further Reading

These are sources that offer many differing points of view and expand on the themes of this book.

Advice on Dying and Living a Better Life, by His Holiness the Dalai Lama. New York: Random House, 2002.

After One-Hundred-And-Twenty: Reflections on Death, Mourning and The Afterlife in The Jewish Tradition, by Hillel Halkin. Princeton, NJ: Princeton University Press, 2016.

The December Project: An Extraordinary Rabbi and a Skeptical Seeker Confront Life's Greatest Mystery, by Sara Davidson (with Rabbi Zalman Schachter-Shalomi). New York: Harper Collins, 2014.

Earth Prayers from Around the World (1991) and *Life Prayers from Around the World* (1996), edited by Elizabeth Roberts and Elias Amidon. San Francisco: HarperSanFrancisco.

Final Last Acts II, by Chris Docker (expanded and revised, 2015), Edinburgh, Scotland. Available through *Exit Euthanasia.* (The Scottish Voluntary Euthanasia Society) www.euthanasia. cc/vess.html

Finding the Words: Candid Conversations with Loved Ones, by Susan Halpern. Berkeley, CA: North Atlantic Books, 2009.

The Five Invitations: Discovering What Death Can Teach Us about Living Fully, by Frank Ostaseski. New York: Flatiron Books, 2017.

The Grace in Dying: A Message of Hope, Comfort, and Spiritual Transformation, (soft cover), by Kathleen Dowling Singh. San Francisco: HarperSanFrancisco, 1998.

I Become Part of It: Sacred Dimensions in Native American Life, edited by D. M. Dooling and Paul Jordan-Smith. New York: Parabola Books, 1989.

The Illustrated World's Religions: A Guide to Our Wisdom Traditions, by Huston Smith. San Francisco: HarperSanFrancisco, 1991.

Life After Death: Contributions by Arnold Toynbee, Arthur Koestler and others. New York: McGraw-Hill, 1976.

Life's Last Gift: Giving and Receiving Peace When a Loved One is Dying, by Charles Garfield. Las Vegas, NV: Central Recovery Press, 2017.

The Myth of the Eternal Return or, Cosmos and History, by Mircea Eliade. Princeton, NJ: Princeton University Press, 1954.

The Perennial Philosophy, by Aldous Huxley. New York: Harper & Brothers, 1945.

Return to Life: Extraordinary Cases of Children Who Remember Past Lives, by Jim B. Tucker. New York: St. Martin's Press, 2013.

The Spiritual Legacy of the American Indian, by Joseph Epes Brown. New York: Crossroad, 1989.

Staring at the Sun: Overcoming the Terror of Death, by Irvin D. Yalom. San Francisco: Jossey-Bass, 2008.

To Pause at the Threshold: Reflections on Living on the Border, by Esther de Waal. Harrisburg, PA: Morehouse Publishing, 2001.

Wisdomkeepers: Meetings with Native American Spiritual Elders, by Steve Wall and Harvey Arden: Hillsboro, OR: Beyond Words Publishing, 1990.

Words at the Threshold: What We Say as We're Nearing Death, by Lisa Smartt. Novato, CA: New World Library, 2017.

Your Legacy Matters: A Multi-generational Guide for Writing Your Ethical Will, by Rachael Freed. Ferndale, MI: Minerva Press, 2013.

Organizational Resources

The Threshold Choir, "Singing gently at the threshold of life in over 150 communities around the world." Contact them for their free services, or if you wish to join. https://thresholdchoir.org

Compassion & Choices, based in Denver, Colorado, offers end-of-life counseling and help with advance planning. www.compassionandchoices.org

Death with Dignity is an organization based in Portland, Oregon that helped craft and pass Oregon's assisted suicide law. Their aim is to foster discussion and legislation throughout the US. www.deathwithdignity.org

Final Exit Network is based in Tallahassee, Florida, and is a national organization that publicly offers education, support, and a compassionate presence to its members. www.finalexitnetwork.org

Resources for writing a legacy letter: https://life-legacies.com

Permissions

Excerpts from *Desert Wisdom* ©2011, reprinted with permission from Neil Douglas-Klotz, author. All rights reserved, including the right to reprint in any form. For information: Abwoon Network at www.abwoon.org

Excerpts from *Staring at the Sun: Overcoming the Terror of Death,* by Irvin D. Yalom, San Francisco: Jossey-Bass, ©2008, through Copyright Clearance Center.

Brief excerpts from pp. 81-2, 90, 94, 110-111, 272 from *The Grace in Dying: How We Are Transformed Spiritually as We Die,* by Kathleen Dowling Singh, ©1998 by Kathleen Dowling Singh. Reprinted by permission of HarperCollins Publishers.

Brief quotes from pp. 6-7, 70, 171 from *The December Project,* by Sara Davidson, ©2014 by Sara Davidson. Reprinted by permission of HarperCollins Publishers.

Quote from website of Threshold Choir used with permission of Connie Curry.

From *Proof of Heaven,* by Eben Alexander, M.D., ©2012 by Eben Alexander, M.D. Reprinted with the permission of Simon & Schuster, Inc. All rights reserved.

Excerpts from *A Personal Encounter with Death and Some Consequences,* essay by Sheldon Ruderman in (anthology) *Between Life and Death,* ©1979, edited by Robert Kastenbaum, used with permission from Springer Publishing Company, through Copyright Clearance Center.

With a Grateful Heart...

My deepest gratitude goes to Charlie Garfield, my husband and soulmate, who has encouraged me every step of the way, and who served as a consultant and editor, a man for all seasons.

With deep appreciation to Valerie Andrews, who applied her fine editing skills to the manuscript and made the writing much clearer and more penetrating.

I want to particularly acknowledge Ned Leavitt, who gently pushed me beyond the unconscious boundaries with which I began this book. He has been invaluable both to the process of this book, and as a mentor on my spiritual journey.

My gratitude also goes to those who shared their personal stories so that others may benefit: Peggy Flynn, Tom Henry, Shams Kairys, and Judith Frank.

Deep appreciation to dear friends who formed a community of reviewers and supporters for me: Elisabeth Belle, Amida Cary, my brother Mark Centkowski, Dan Drasin, Karin Evans, Shelli Fried, Judith Frank, Patti Hamel, Susan Halpern, Jane Hoover, Bharat Lindemood, Molly Reno, my cousin Mary Spry, Frances Vaughan, Roger Walsh, Mimi Zemmelman, and Steve Zemmelman.

And to conversation providers who encouraged me along the way: Loren Haralson, Judith Frank, Jan Thomas, Peggy Flynn, Kaushik and Stacy Roy, and Janet Ottenweller.

Humble gratitude to those who gave me testimonials: Leonard Joy, Gabriella Lettini, Kate Munger, Frank Ostaseski, Rachel Remen, Frances Vaughan, and Roger Walsh.

For insights that inform this book from Joseph Campbell, Neil Douglas-Klotz, His Holiness the Dalai Lama, Aldous Huxley, Elizabeth Roberts, Kathleen Dowling Singh, Arnold Toynbee, Huston Smith, Roger Walsh, and Irvin Yalom.

For teaching me more about death during the writing of this book, my beloved cats Snooky and Arthur Pendragon. The photo of me on the back cover was taken in front of the apple tree that was nourished by Snooky's ashes. It was taken by an extraordinary photographer and my dear friend, Stu Selland.

And to the midwives whose labors helped bring this book into the larger world:

Self-publishing consultant Naomi Rose, who held my hand firmly during the long post-manuscript process.

Cover, interior design, and layout by Margaret Copeland of Terragrafix, whose beautiful work is the first and last thing you see when you read this book.

Jane Hayes, whose perfect painting graces the cover of this book, and who generously donated it to me.

About the Author

Cindy Spring is an author, social activist, and explorer of the unconventional. She authored *Wisdom Circles: A Guide to Self-Discovery and Community Building in Small Groups* (Hyperion, 1998), and co-authored with Charles Garfield *Sometimes My Heart Goes Numb: Love and Caregiving in a Time of AIDS* (Jossey-Bass, 1995). She co-edited the anthology *Earthlight: Spiritual Wisdom for an Ecological Age* (Friends Bulletin, 2007). She was also a national producer of over one hundred nonfiction audiobooks.

Since the mid-1990s, she has been active in local ecology in the San Francisco area, co-founding two ecology nonprofits, EarthTeam and Close to Home: Exploring Nature in the East Bay, as well as serving as coordinator for Earth Day 2000 for the Bay Area. Her explorations have been in the fields of spirituality, transpersonal psychology, and personal growth. She lives in Northern California with her husband Charlie and two cats, Bella and Layla.

Author's Note

I encourage you to discuss the insights you gain from this book in a circle with others. The wisdom-circle format provides a guide for deep sharing in the context of listening and speaking from the heart. See www.wisdom-circles.org for how to begin.

To contact me, please email: wave@cindyspring.com.

Printed in the USA
CPSIA information can be obtained
at www.ICGtesting.com
LVHW102112010823
753870LV00010B/925